Speak,

Listen,

Communicate!

Speak, Listen, Communicate!

MERRITT B. JONES
Manatee Junior College

 D. VAN NOSTRAND COMPANY

New York • Cincinnati • Toronto • London • Melbourne

(Photograph by Walter Holt, courtesy of Bryn Mawr College.)

D. Van Nostrand Company Regional Offices:
New York   Cincinnati

D. Van Nostrand Company International Offices:
London   Toronto   Melbourne

Published by D. Van Nostrand Company
135 West 50th Street, New York, N.Y. 10020

10   9   8   7   6   5   4   3   2   1

Preface

Speak, Listen, Communicate! discusses interpersonal communication as well as the performance aspects of speech communication: speech improvement, group discussion, parliamentary procedure, public speaking, and persuasion. The book is intended as a core text for a one- or two-semester college course in speech communication. It is especially designed for a course in the fundamentals of speech, but is also suitable for courses in group discussion or public speaking.

The materials in *Speak, Listen, Communicate!* are presented in logical order, from theory to application. Instructors who wish to exclude certain chapters or to assign chapters in a different sequence will find it practical to do so since each chapter is more or less self-contained. In addition, each chapter is followed by a list of practical projects that illustrate and review the theory presented in the chapter. The instructor may want to assign some or all of these projects.

Speak, Listen, Communicate! is student-oriented. It "talks" to students. It is concerned with their problems, accomplishments, and goals. It covers the information essential to an understanding of the communication process and includes numerous suggestions for applying the information in the questionnaires, various personal inventories, worksheets, drills, and group projects provided. Thus, *Speak, Listen, Communicate!* aids the student in better understanding speech communication and acquiring skill at communicating.

v

Each chapter is preceded by a list of performance objectives. These objectives give students an indication of the content and purpose of each chapter and a preview of the major ideas covered. For students who wish to study a particular topic in depth, each chapter is followed by an up-to-date annotated list of suggested readings.

Contents

Part Two. Group Discussion 127

11. Parliamentary Procedure   183

Part Three.   Public Speaking   197

12. Planning Your Speech   199

Introduction

In today's topsy-turvy world of rising inflation, high unemployment, social unrest, and constant threats of devastating global war, "communication breakdown" is often cited as a factor contributing to these social ills. If this is the case, we should be greatly concerned about the failures and inadequacies of our communication and we should take drastic steps to remedy the situation.

"Communication breakdown" can mean many things, but basically it means that one person or group fails to understand another person or group—that there has been a derailment of the communication process, a failure to communicate. And communication breakdown can occur in any form of communication whether it is speaking, writing, electronic broadcasting, semaphore, or even smoke signals.

This book deals with one very important aspect of communication—speech. It is important because 75 percent of all communication is speech communication—speaking and listening—and yet many of us accept our speech inadequacies, our poor listening habits, our communication breakdowns with a fatalistic shrug. We think we were born that way. Not so! Speech communication is a learned behavior. We can become just as skilled in speech communication as in any other activity—swimming, dancing, reading, writing, calculus, you name it!

And so, this book is concerned with speech communication—speaking and listening. It is not written as a comprehensive encyclopedia, but it does attempt to cover the basic concepts of effective com-

1

munication and the development of skills needed in certain communication activities such as interpersonal communication, group discussion, and public speaking.

The book is divided into a logical sequence beginning with the theory of speech communication followed by an explanation and practice of the special forms of communication. Also, the materials are arranged in order of difficulty, from easy to more difficult assignments.

Part One of the text, Basic Principles of Speech Communication, discusses the theory of speech communication. Chapter 1 gives an overview of the function and nature of speech communication with special emphasis on speech communication models. Chapter 2 deals with the individual as communicator and stresses the concept of building personality through communication. Chapter 3 explores the use of language, both verbal and nonverbal, which is essential to effective communication. Chapters 4 and 5 discuss sound production, pronunciation, dictionary usage, and speech delivery and include many practice drills. Chapter 6 covers the important function of hearing and listening and chapter 7 discusses the concepts of interpersonal communication and gives practical suggestions on interviewing.

Part Two, Discussion, begins with a chapter on logic followed by two chapters on group discussion and one on parliamentary procedure.

Part Three, Public Speaking, covers the area of public speaking in four chapters: planning the speech, developing the speech, presenting the speech, and persuasive speaking.

The Appendix includes various critique forms, additional projects, and other materials. *To begin:* Complete both sides of the self-inventory sheet in the Appendix, and hand it in to your instructor. He or she will want to know something about your background and may want to contact you at home sometime. Also, since much of your work in this course will be of an interpersonal nature and involve communication with your classmates, it is essential that you get acquainted as soon as possible. The ice-breaker projects in the Appendix are designed for this purpose. Let's get acquainted!

Part One

Basic Principles of Speech Communication

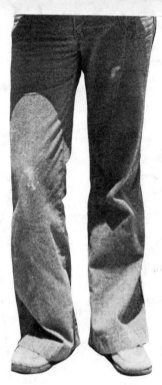

"SPEECH IS CIVILIZATION ITSELF

Thomas Mann

Photograph by Jerald W. Rogers.

Chapter 1

The Function and Nature of Speech Communication

Performance Objectives

After studying chapter 1, you should be able to:

1. Describe the major functions of speech communication.
2. Define speech communication.
3. Explain intrapersonal communication.
4. Explain interpersonal communication.
5. Explain the difference between verbal and nonverbal language.
6. Explain the function of a speech communication model.
7. Define the variables listed in our speech communication model.
8. Explain the relationship between referent, reference, and symbol.
9. Formulate your own concept of a speech communication model.
10. Analyze a hypothetical conversation using the variables of your model.

"Let your fingers do the walking!" Good slogan! Good idea! Finger-walking—reading—is just fine but talking and listening are also important. And that's what this book is all about: talking and listening. Communicating. But before we get too involved in our favorite topic, speech communication, let us briefly examine the term "communication" itself. The word "communication" is somewhat ambiguous. It can mean a connection between mechanical parts, such as a drive-shaft on an automobile; the transference of electrical energy to a kitchen appliance; a connecting highway between two cities; or the effect of one organism on another organism.

We can narrow the concept quite a bit by using only the last definition of communication: that it is the effect of one organism on another organism. It is generally agreed that many animals communicate. It is probable that dolphins, for example, have a fairly complex system of communication. And we are all familiar with the various communication attempts of our household pets, from the contented purr of Tabby, the cat, to the ferocious warning growl of Bowser, the dog.

Of course, we would be on even more familiar ground if we limited the concept of communication to *human* communication. Even this narrower concept would cover quite a range of communication forms: the written message, the spoken message, the use of electronic media, and the use of codes such as verbal, Morse, and semaphore. *Human communication,* then, is the conscious or unconscious modification of another person's behavior through the use of various signals and symbols perceived through the senses of that other person.

With this rather general introduction to communication and human communication, let us now return to our special concern—speech communication.

THE FUNCTIONS OF SPEECH COMMUNICATION

We will consider the functions, purposes, or goals of speech communication for a single communicator (intrapersonal), a pair of communicators (interpersonal), a small interacting group (interpersonal), and finally, a one-to-many situation including mass-media communication.

Intrapersonal communication

Intrapersonal communication is that self-communication that takes place within the individual with no other communicators participating. Although this type of communication may not meet the criteria of our definition of speech communication, we cannot entirely ignore it. Certainly the lone communicator formulates mental symbols and goes through the process of stimulation, perception, and message formulation. An individual may mentally work on and solve a particular problem; plan a future activity; participate in an imaginary, unspoken dialogue. After all, "The thought is the mother of the word; the word is mother of the act." Our lone communicator may also daydream, fantasize, or have a jumble of unrelated thoughts. Whatever the type of thought and intraverbalization, it is a form of communication. Many people, especially if isolated from others for long periods of time, will even talk aloud to themselves or to animals, which could be classified as speech communication of a sort.

One-to-one or interpersonal communication

The purposes of dyadic communication, communication between two people, are myriad. We can only classify some of the purposes in a general way:

To satisfy wants. "Please pass the butter"; "I'll have the Surf 'n Turf"; "Fill 'er up!"; "Are you busy tonight?"

To gain information. "Is this the road to Venice?"; "What time does the library close?"; "Do you have a car for sale?"

To entertain. "What are you doing these days, Thumbs?" "Same old thing—brain surgery."

To strengthen belief. "You really owe it to yourself to finish college; you will never regret it."

To change belief. "Most doctors agree that smoking is bad for your health."

To socialize. "How are you today?"; "Beautiful day!"; "Have a good day!"

The replies or responses to the purposes listed above—to satisfy the wants of another, to give information, to respond to entertainment, to respond to persuasive communication, and to reciprocate the social message—are also functions of one-to-one speech communication.

Small group or interpersonal communication

The functions of speech communication in a small group situation parallel, to a considerable extent, the functions of one-to-one communication. Individuals in small groups may satisfy their wants, gain information, entertain, persuade, socialize, and so on, or they may respond to similar communication purposes from others in the group. However, there are some specific small groups that have one or more particular functions. For example, in the classroom situation, the teacher attempts to instruct the students or modify their behavior patterns. In a discussion group, the functions of the group may be to exchange information; to reduce friction between opposing factions, for example, labor–management; to formulate policy, as in a management group; or to solve problems, as in a governmental, business, or civic group. (See our chapters on group discussion.) Some small groups, such as committees, may meet in a communication situation to perform some special function for a larger group.

There are many occasions when a small group of people from government, civic, educational, or social organizations meet together to discuss a need or to solve a problem.*

One-to-many or mass communication

The function of speech communication in one-to-many situations includes the informative or behavioral-modification function of the typical classroom teacher; the informative, entertaining, persua-

*It is quite difficult to define "small group." However, for our present purposes we will define the term as a group of three to twenty in which all members can actively participate.

Speak, listen, communicate! (Courtesy of Adelphi University)

sive functions of the public speaker; and the inspirational function of some speakers, for example, the religious speaker. Finally, in mass communication situations such as radio, television, motion pictures, and the theater, all functions of speech communication are used to inform, to entertain, to inspire, to persuade.

We summarize our discussion of the function of speech communication by considering some of the more important purposes of human speech communication: giving and receiving information, persuading others, and improving human relationships.

Giving and receiving information

Speaking–listening is our primary method of giving and receiving information. We instruct, assist, and advise our fellow humans with speech; we learn new skills, vital knowledge, important concepts by listening to others speak. This ability to communicate our thoughts and feelings by the use of symbols is the most important feature distinguishing humans from other creatures because with it we can transmit knowledge from one generation to the next. This means that we can learn and benefit from events and discoveries that took place hundreds of years ago. Time is bridged and history is our teacher.

Persuading others

Speech communication is our chief means of modifying the behavior of others, either to strengthen or change belief. The salesman sells a product, the legislator gains support for a bill, the diplomat promotes a country's policies through speech communication.

On a more personal level, we persuade through speech when we apply for a job, when we suggest vacation plans to our families, or when we ask a friend to join us for lunch. Persuasion through speech is a continual and important part of daily living.

Improving human relationships

Speech communication is the obvious means of improving human relationships. We exchange pleasantries, points of view, and inquiries about mutual problems with our friends and associates. This small talk gives us a sense of belonging, of being aware that we are all members of the human race with common needs and common problems. Speech makes social togetherness practical, or, as Thomas Mann said, "Speech is civilization itself."

> Speech communication is our best means of
> giving and receiving information,
> persuading others, and
> improving human relationships.

THE NATURE OF SPEECH COMMUNICATION

Speech communication is the process of using spoken verbal symbols (words) and nonverbal symbols such as gestures and facial expressions to make known our thoughts and feelings to other people—or even to our pet dog or cat. With our speech organs we produce certain sounds in a prescribed sequence. This constitutes language. We utter these sound combinations—words, phrases, or sentences—at a certain pitch, rate, and loudness level so that our message is audible and comprehensible to our listeners. If our listeners seem to understand our message and nod their heads (or wag their tails), voilà! We have communicated.

> Speech communication is the process
> by which the thoughts and feelings
> of one person are conveyed, by
> verbal and nonverbal symbols, to
> one or more persons.

On the surface, this seems to be a fairly simple process, but it is actually quite complex. There are many factors, or variables, in the communication process that must be carefully controlled in order to achieve effective communication. Let's consider just a few of these variables.

1. The *language* used in communicating must be common to both the speaker and the listener. If the speaker speaks in a tongue foreign to the listener, the intended message is gibberish. It evokes no meaning in the mind of the listener. Communication does not take place when the speaker uses French and the listener understands only German.
2. On the other hand, using a common language does not ensure satis-

factory communication. The *vocabulary* of the speaker's message must be appropriate to the comprehension level of the listener. An argument directed at a William Buckley may well be too difficult for an eighth-grader to understand.

3. The speaker must speak loudly enough to be heard.
4. The speaker must not speak too rapidly to be understood.
5. The speaker's pronunciation must be understood and accepted by the listener. If the speaker's pronunciation varies too far from standard pronunciation, it will be misunderstood and the communication attempt will falter.
6. The speaker's nonverbal communication must agree with his or her verbal communication. If the nonverbal message contradicts the verbal message, the listener will be unsure of the speaker's intent.
7. Interference, such as physical noise, inattention, and distance, must be kept at a minimum. Too much interference will negate the communication intent.

These are just a few of the many factors involved in successful communication, but they indicate that speech communication is not simple. On the contrary, it is highly complex.

First of all, speech communication is a process. Adult A communicates to adult B one bit of information. This "drop" of information, modified by the immediate situation and the total environment, is added to the billions of other "drops" of information received during B's lifetime. This particular communication is thus a tiny part of a continuing process. It may reinforce B's concept of reality or it may alter B's concept. In any event, the communication is a process; that is, a continuing phenomenon.

Speech communication is ongoing and everchanging. As Heraclitus, the Greek, said, "One can never step in the same river twice." It is the same with speech.

Also, we must keep in mind that, unlike written messages, when we speak many communication factors occur at the same time. For example, a speaker may utter a few words and at the same time gesture, change stance, look into the eyes of the listener, and be planning the next sentence. And, at the same time, the listener may be reacting in a similar multi-activity fashion. Although in reality it is impossible to isolate a given speech factor from the overall communication situation, we can do so artificially with various speech models. A study of speech models may also give us some additional insight into the complexities of speech communication.

SPEECH COMMUNICATION MODELS

A model is a representation of something. It attempts to describe or show, in shortened form, something relatively complex. We are all familiar with model toys or miniatures, such as those of cars, boats, and airplanes. These are concrete, or material, models. But models may also be pictorial, such as a wiring diagram, or verbal, such as the table of contents of a book. In some instances, a model may be a combination of both pictorial and verbal representations; see Figure 1–3, for example.

Some advantages of studying a speech communication model are that:

1. It gives us a simplified version of a complex process;
2. It enables us to isolate a particular communication variable so that we may discuss it with others; and
3. It serves as a starting point for research on one or more variables of a given communication.

One of the early verbal models of speech communication was Aristotle's concept of public speaking as *speaker, speech, audience,* and *effect.* A modern version of this idea is found in Lasswell's model (Figure 1–1).[1]

David Berlo devised a speech communication model in 1960 that was somewhat more detailed than Lasswell's model. Berlo's model consists of four major variables, *source, message, channel,* and *receiver,* each subdivided into appropriate categories (see Figure 1–2).[2] The Berlo model, though quite useful for many communication situations, has some drawbacks. It omits the concepts of feedback and interference and it fails to show the relationship of the various communication factors and the circular nature of communication. Our model is more detailed. It is impossible, however, to list all of the many variables that might occur in speech communication situations.

Who
Says What
In Which Channel
To Whom
With What Effect?

FIGURE 1–1.
Lasswell's model.

The speech communication model shown in Figure 1–3 represents the setting, or stage, for a one-to-one communication, as in a conversation. Note that many *possible* variables are indicated. Whether they are all used depends upon the particular situation. For example, we have indicated "interference" on the model. If there is no interference in a communication instance, then that variable would not apply.

When studying the model, realize that speech communication is a dynamic, ongoing, everchanging process. Understand, also, that a model is only a partial *representation*. A model is never actuality.

EXPLAINING OUR MODEL

Figure 1–3, p. 14 shows speech communication as a circular process. So, theoretically, if we wished to discuss a particular aspect of communication, we could begin anywhere on the model: with the person initiating the communication (the source), with the listener (receiver), or even with the feedback from the listener. For our purposes, we will begin our explanation with the stimulus to the source of the message. In our model, we have shown the stimulus as an external

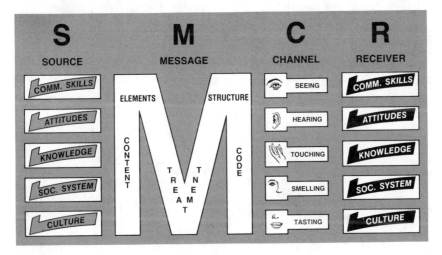

FIGURE 1–2.
Berlo's model.*

*From *The Process of Communication: An Introduction to Theory and Practice* by David K. Berlo. Copyright (c) 1960 by Holt, Rinehart and Winston, Inc. Reprinted by permission of Holt, Rinehart and Winston.

14

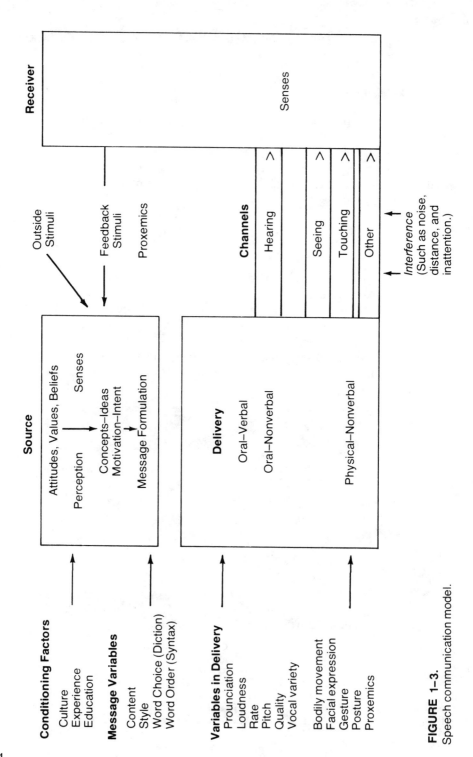

FIGURE 1-3.
Speech communication model.

factor, for example, an object or an event. However, the stimulus to communicate could also be internal; that is, within the communicator: a physiological need (such as hunger or thirst) or a psychological want (such as affection).

Before we proceed with our explanation of the model, let's look at the relationship of the stimulus to the communicator. This relationship is shown in Figure 1–4. Observe that in Figure 1–4 the stimulus, or object, when noted by the communicator's senses, *causes* a perception of the object in the mind of the communicator. This perception, plus a desire, or motivation, to share the observation, *causes* the communicators to formulate their perceptions as a word or words. Note that there is a causal relation between the object and the perception and a causal relation between the perception and the word but there is no direct relationship between the word and the object. In other words, *the word is not the thing.* Although everyone really knows this, sometimes people tend to react to a word as though it were, indeed, the object itself.

Figure 1–4 shows that sources, or speakers, receive a stimulus through their senses that results in perception or recognition of an object or event. This perception is modified or added to by the speakers' attitudes, values, and beliefs, which have in turn been molded by the various conditioning factors of the speakers' experiences, education, and cultural background. At this point, the speakers wish to communicate their observations or mental concepts to other people. They therefore mentally form messages concerning their concepts. The messages are in the form of language; that is, they are in meaningful verbal symbols. The mental messages are now vocalized, including both verbal and oral nonverbal symbols. (The vocalized messages may or may not be accompanied by the visible symbols of body language.) The vocalized messages, including the many variables of delivery such as

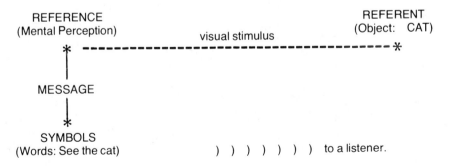

FIGURE 1–4.
Referent, reference, symbol.

pronunciation, loudness, rate, pitch, bodily movement, and so on, are "broadcast" through the air or other media (for example, the telephone) to the ears and other sense organs of the receivers. The "broadcast," which is subject to various forms of interference, such as noise, distance, and inattention, must now be translated by the receivers into meaningful thought and idea patterns. When this is accomplished, the receivers will respond in some verbal or nonverbal manner. This response is called feedback. The nature of the feedback will influence the continuity of the communication. If a receiver replies, "I don't understand," for example, the speaker will no doubt restate his communication in simpler terms. At this point, the communication may cease or it may continue its circular process. In any event, the effects of the communication will probably endure.

How would this communication process work in a real-life situation? Let us assume that the model represents the communication setting for two people: Joe **(source)** and Betty **(receiver).*** They are looking for a friend in a shopping center. Joe sees **(outside stimuli to his senses)** a person in the distance whom he **perceives** as their friend. Joe,

*The words and phrases in boldface type refer to the variables listed in the model.

influenced in part by his **attitudes, values, and beliefs,** which in turn have been formed by his **cultural background, experiences, and education,** wants **(is motivated)** to tell Betty **(intent)** that he sees their friend. In his mind he **formulates a message,** using selected word symbols **(diction)** in a certain order **(syntax),** which he utters aloud **(verbal and nonverbal oral delivery)** as follows: "There she is now, going into the bookstore." When delivering this message to Betty, Joe **pronounces** each word in a prescribed manner, with adequate **loudness,** at a comprehensible **rate,** using a normal adult male **pitch** and **tonal quality,** with a degree of **vocal variety.** As he speaks, he turns **(bodily movement)** to Betty, smiles **(facial expression),** turns **(bodily movement)** in the other direction, and points **(gestures)** toward the friend. As he speaks, his **posture** is one of animation, and he leans toward Betty **(proxemics) touching** her arm. Joe's **message** is **delivered** to Betty vocally and physically, via the channels of **hearing, seeing, and touching,** to Betty's ears, eyes, and sense of touch. But, alas! As Joe speaks, a big truck rumbles by **(interference)** and Betty asks, "What did you say, Joe?" **(feedback)** Joe repeats his **message** using a greater degree of **loudness** and a slower **rate.** (Note that communication is self-correcting.) Eureka! Betty gets the message and sees their friend.

A model helps us visualize and understand the process of speech communication.

Projects

1. Discuss, in small groups, additional functions of speech communication in small and large groups, for example, legislative bodies. Be prepared to share your findings with the class.
2. Prepare a speech model of your own depicting a three-way discussion (a triad). You may wish to accentuate a particular concept or indicate a particular element of a complex communication. Be original.
3. Present a short written segment of a real-life conversation and indicate what variables are being used.
4. In your own terms, define your concept of speech communication. Be as complete as necessary for understanding.

Notes

1. Harold Lasswell, "The Structure and Function of Communication in Society." From *The Communication of Ideas*, L. Bryson, ed., (New York: Harper and Row, 1948), p. 37. Reprinted by permission of Harper and Row, Inc.
2. David K. Berlo, *The Process of Communication: An Introduction to Theory and Practice*. (New York: Holt, Rinehart and Winston, 1960), p. 77.

Suggested Readings

Dance, Frank E. X. and Carl E. Larsen, *Speech Communication, Concepts and Behaviors*, (New York: Holt, Rinehart, and Winston, 1972).

See Chapters 1–3, which contain an excellent summary of speech communication models, including those of Shannon and Weaver, Lasswell, Berlo, and Baker. The authors carefully define the term "communication" and list thirteen basic designs for speech communication.

McCroskey, James C. and James R. Wheeless, *Introduction to Human Communication*, (Boston: Allyn and Bacon, 1976).

The first two chapters of Introduction to Human Communication present an overview of human communication and set the stage for the subjects covered in the remainder of the book. The style of this book is direct and student-oriented. Of special interest to the student is the discussion of common misconceptions about communication.

Mortensen, C. David, *Communication: The Study of Human Interaction,* (New York: McGraw-Hill, 1972).

This text is aimed at the speech communication major. Chapter 1 defines communication in considerable depth. It includes an interesting model of the various systems in communication, including intrapersonal, interpersonal, and sociocultural systems. Models are used extensively in Chapter 2 to recreate the various aspects of speech communication.

Webb, Ralph Jr., *Interpersonal Communication: Principles and Practices,* (Englewood Cliffs, N.J.: Prentice-Hall, 1975).

The first pages of this book present a fine discussion of the basic elements of speech communication. Included are a contrast of sign and symbol, the distinguishing features of speech, levels of communication, and a thorough treatment of speech models. This book is highly recommended.

TO THINE OWN SELF
BE TRUE

Photograph by Jerald W. Rogers.

Chapter 2

Individuals as Communicators

After studying chapter 2, you should be able to:

1. Explain the four basic determinants of individual characteristics and growth.
2. Explain the terms *personality, character, and individuality.*
3. Itemize the observable and unobservable aspects of personality.
4. Define the following concepts: *values, attitudes, beliefs.*
5. Explain the Johari Window.
6. Explain the eight "personalities" involved in a one-to-one conversation.
7. Define *self-actualization.*
8. Explain and comment on the eight positive steps toward self-actualization.

"Who says what to whom?" was a part of one of the speech communication models mentioned in the previous chapter.[1] This question is our present concern. Who is *who*? And who is *whom*? The first (the person who initiates the communication) is called the source of the message and the second (the person who gets the message) is called the receiver. And then, if there is a response, the roles are reversed and Number 2 becomes the source and Number 1 the receiver. In this chapter, we will examine the *what, when, where,* and *why* of the *who* and *whom*—the individuals as communicators.

An overworked professor, speaking of his 300 students said, "Well, they all look alike to me." A joke, maybe? But we know that every person is different, unique, one of a kind—even an identical twin. The differences—physical, mental, emotional, social—are due to many factors. Let's examine the basic determinants of differences in individuals and the impact of communication on them.

THE BASIC DETERMINANTS OF INDIVIDUAL CHARACTERISTICS AND DIFFERENCES

Heredity

Individuals inherit certain genetic traits from their parents at conception. These traits determine to a considerable extent the individuals' physical characteristics: skin color, hair texture, body build. The genetic factor may also include potentialities for the development of certain skills and kinds of behavior. For example, the infant has the potential ability to walk, run, and speak. Heredity is also probably involved in such traits as intelligence, sensitivity, vigor, and temperament.[2]

Environment

We will divide *environment* into three categories: (1) physical, (2) social, and (3) cultural. Let us briefly look at these as they relate to the development of the individual.

The physical environment refers to the climate, terrain, availability of food, proximity to water, and so on. This factor obviously does have an effect on human development, although in this country, with its great abundance of natural resources and modern methods of transportation, the effect is not as apparent as it might be in some areas of the world.

The social, or group environment of nation, state, community, family, and other groups, has considerable impact on the development of the individual. Families "humanize" infants, teaching them (often unintentionally) a way of life, introducing them to group living, teaching them to walk, talk, use a spoon, "mind Mama," and so on. In a few years, infants learn games, sports, attitudes, and beliefs from their peers. Then the schools and other institutions will further mold the individual. Indeed, though patterns may not always be the same, individuals are influenced from the moment of their birth to their dying day.

The cultural environment is linked with the societal environment. *Culture* refers to the folkways, customs, language, mores, laws, and other ways of life of a particular society. These ways of life are learned by all members of the culture.

The concept of self

Another very important determinant of individuality is the concept of self. At a very early age, individuals have a realization of self. They develop individualities based on their concepts of reality, their needs, and their acquired values. It is important to the growth of individuals that they have a sense of self and feel a sense of personal worth. Self-understanding and self-approval are the first steps toward becoming a well-adjusted, fully functioning person. These goals are called self-realization or self-actualization.*

In communication, we are especially concerned about two of these determinants of individuals: their sociocultural environments and their concepts of self. These two determinants can be modified or used, for the betterment of individuals. They can impel individuals toward goals of physical, mental, and emotional growth—self-actualization.

EFFECTS OF THE SOCIOCULTURAL ENVIRONMENT ON THE INDIVIDUAL

"As the twig is bent, so grows the tree." There is little doubt that we are creatures of our environment. We are conditioned from birth by our families, friends, teachers, peers, and society at large. The following poem by Dorothy Law Nolte emphasizes this conditioning concept.

*The term self-actualization is usually associated with Abraham Maslow but was probably coined by Kurt Goldstein in *The Organism,* (New York: The American Book Company, 1939).

Children Learn What They Live

If a child lives with criticism
  He learns to condemn
If a child lives with hostility
  He learns to fight
If a child lives with ridicule
  He learns to be shy
If a child lives with shame
  He learns to feel guilty
If a child lives with tolerance
  He learns to be patient
If a child lives with encouragement
  He learns confidence
If a child lives with praise
  He learns to appreciate
If a child lives with fairness
  He learns justice
If a child lives with security
  He learns to have faith
If a child lives with approval
  He learns to like himself
If a child lives with acceptance and friendship
  He learns to find love in the world.

In other words, we develop certain traits or characteristics from environmental conditioning. And what is the nature of these traits or characteristics? Some may be desirable, some undesirable; some refer to actions, others to feelings. In general, we are speaking of *personality* traits, which, in a broad sense, may be defined as the total make-up of a human being, including physical, emotional, mental, and social attributes. However, it might be helpful to distinguish "personality" from "character" and "individuality" as follows:

Personality refers particularly to the outer and inner characteristics that determine the impression one makes.

Character refers especially to moral qualities, ethical standards, principles, and the like.

Individuality refers to the distinctive qualities that make one recognizable as a person differentiated from others.

PERSONALITY

In this chapter we are especially concerned with understanding the nature and acquisition of *personality*. Coleman suggests the following classification of traits as a determinant of individual personality differences.[3]*

1. *Physical appearance,* or physique, hair color, eye color, facial features, and other characteristics of bodily equipment.
2. *Temperament,* or prevailing mood pattern.
3. *Capacity,* or potential for development in a given area.
4. *Ability,* or actual competency or skill of performance in a given area.
5. *Interest,* or degree of attraction toward any activity.
6. *Attitude,* or a propensity to react in a given way, (for example, favorably, unfavorably, cautiously) to a given object or situation.
7. *Aptitude,* or a propensity for doing well in a particular area of activity, (for example, in medicine or law).
8. *Character,* or the moral and ethical dimensions of personality.
9. *Stress tolerance,* or level of resistance to physical and psychological stress.
10. *Action patterns,* or broadly characteristic ways of interacting with one's environment (for example, as an extrovert or introvert, aggressively or submissively).

Another approach to a classification of personality that might be more suitable for the study of communication is separating the subject into observable aspects of personality, and unobservable aspects of personality.

Observable aspects of personality

1. Physical appearance.
2. Physical movement. Is the individual graceful or awkward, hurried or deliberate?
3. Acts (behavior patterns). Things the individual does or did.

*From *Personality Dynamics and Effective Behavior* by James Coleman. Copyright© 1960 by Scott, Foresman and Company. Reprinted by permission.

4. Dress and grooming. Is the individual formal or casual, neat or sloppy?
5. Speech
   a. Content of message
   b. Delivery
      (1) Verbal
      (2) Nonverbal

Unobservable aspects of personality

1. Intelligence
2. Knowledge
3. Education
4. Emotional sensitivity
5. Values
6. Attitudes
7. Beliefs

These traits and others, are often revealed by speech.

Values, attitudes, beliefs

Since values, attitudes, and beliefs are important and often misunderstood aspects of personality, we will define and differentiate them. Notice that there is a close relationship between values and attitudes.

Values are the beliefs a society holds about what is good and what is bad. A society may, for example, put a positive value on cleanliness, freedom, and education and a negative value on cruelty, theft, and atheism. An *attitude* is a predisposition or tendency to evaluate or respond to a person, thing, or phenomenon in a certain manner, favorable or unfavorable. We have many attitudes, some of which are strongly held, whereas others may be temporary or approaching neutral. Examples of attitude questions are: "What is your attitude toward capital punishment?" "What is your attitude toward legalizing marijuana?" *Beliefs* are concepts about factual matters; that is, whether some person, thing, or phenomenon exists or did exist. A belief is confidence in the truth of something that cannot be immediately confirmed; an opinion.

In general, values and attitudes have to do with what is good or bad, right or wrong, desirable or undesirable. Values are comparatively few and quite enduring, whereas attitudes are numerous. (Some Americans have an attitude about almost everything.) Attitudes may be based on values and are probably more subject to change than are values. Steele and Redding, in a 1962 article in *Western Speech,* present a list of core values shared by many Americans:[4]

1. *Puritan and pioneer morality.* Americans have a tendency to view the world in moral terms. Things are good or bad, ethical or unethical. This value would encompass "such virtues as continence, honesty, simplicity, cooperation, self-discipline, courage, orderliness, personal responsibility, and humility."

2. *The value of the individual.* A belief in the importance, dignity, and uniqueness of every individual is shared by most Americans.

3. *Achievement and success.* The value of achievement and success stresses material wealth and competetiveness softened with moral effort and personal charity.

4. *Change and progress.* Most Americans are optimistic about the future and believe that "the best is yet to be, and nothing is impossible."

5. *Ethical equality.* The ideal of spiritual equality for all in the eyes of God is the value of ethical equality. This value is demonstrated by free schools and the right to vote.

6. *Equality of opportunity.* Although wealth tends to be unevenly distributed, we still strongly uphold the concept of equal *opportunity* for all Americans.

7. *Effort and optimism.* Hard work and perseverence will overcome all obstacles.

8. *Efficiency, practicality, and pragmatism.* Practical thinkers and doers are held in higher regard than are artists and intellectuals.

9. *Rejection of authority.* Americans want freedom from restraint by government or society.

10. *Science and secular rationality.* Americans have faith in reason, clarity, and order.

THE IMPACT OF COMMUNICATION ON THE INDIVIDUAL

So far we have been concerned with the development and growth of the individual and the concept of personality. Communication, especially speech communication, is an integral part of the conditioning process of molding the personality of an individual. In other words, speech communication is the major tool used in building and modifying personality. The culture of the group—its way of living, values, attitudes, beliefs, customs, manners, and so on—is passed on to the individual through speech, for the most part. Imitation is a type of nonverbal communication. Parents and older siblings talk to children from the children's earliest days. If the talk is gentle, reassuring, and generally supportive, the children's personalities will reflect that attitude. If the talk is harsh, angry, and abusive, the children's personalities will reflect those characteristics. And as children grow older, the process of communication, imitation, and reaction continues until, at a certain age, children begin to be selective, analytical, and critical. The self is emerging and beginning to supplement the sociocultural input. This is the process of personality development. Speech communication is inextricably woven into the educational pattern.

> Speech communication is the major
> tool used in personality development.

The individual communicator. (Courtesy of New York University)

The material covered so far should give you an idea of the factors involved in forming the individual personality. Assuming that you now have some understanding of the conditioning variables that have made you what you are today, we hope that you learn to accept the things about yourself that you cannot change and that you work to modify any undesirable traits that can be changed.

The many faces of Eve

Although we have previously defined personality as the total traits of an individual, it is also typical for a person to use only certain traits for a particular purpose or occasion. In some instances we are aware that we are using a certain set of traits (role playing), but in other instances, we are unaware of the "personality" we are displaying and we are surprised when a particular trait or set of traits is called to our attention. Joseph Luft and Harry Ingram, in 1955, devised a four-category concept of an individual's open and closed personality traits called "Johari's Window."[5] The four categories were: characteristics of an individual known by self and others; characteristics known by self but not by others; characteristics known by others but not by self; and characteristics known by neither self nor others.

We are generally aware that we have personality traits known by self and others, and that we have traits known only to ourselves— secrets. We are less aware that there are aspects of our personality that are known to others but not to ourselves. Ideally, we should know everything about our own personality traits and we should determine to what extent we want others to know our personality traits.

Another approach to the concept of "multipersonality" is demonstrated by the possible personalities in a one-to-one conversation. Let's eavesdrop.

JOE COLLEGE:	Hi, Beautiful. What's new?
BETTY BRIGHT:	Same old thing—brain surgery.
JOE:	What d' you mean? I don't get it.
BETTY:	It's an old joke. What's new with you?
JOE:	Fun and games. Just like always.
BETTY:	Yes, I know.
JOE:	What's that supposed to mean?
BETTY:	You'll get it, but it may take some time.

Now, Table 2–1 examines the "possible personalities" *perceived* by Joe and Betty in the above exchange.

TABLE 2–1. Perceived personalities.

The Personalities of Joe	The Personalities of Betty
Joe's concept of Joe.	Betty's concept of Betty.
Betty's concept of Joe.	Joe's concept of Betty.
Joe's concept of Betty's concept of him.	Betty's concept of Joe's concept of her.
The real, total Joe.	The real, total Betty.

How others react to you is a good indicator of your personality.

SELF-ACTUALIZATION

The term "self-actualization" (realizing our full potential) is usually associated with Abraham Maslow's "hierarchy of man's needs."[6] Maslow's hierarchy can be diagramed as shown in Figure 2–1.

Maslow's hierarchy represents man's needs and wants. Notice that the physiological needs on the lowest line represent life essentials. Maslow says, quite logically, that we must satisfy the basic needs and wants. In other words, we proceed from the bottom of the triangle upward to the top, which is self-actualization. Self-actualization may be equated with self-fulfillment, the fully functioning self, or realizing one's greatest potential. We are concerned, at this point, with understanding and using this concept of self-actualization.

Maslow describes the characteristics of "healthy people" who have

SELF-ACTUALIZATION

ESTEEM AND SELF-RESPECT

BELONGINGNESS AND LOVE NEEDS

SECURITY, ORDER, AND STABILITY

SATISFACTION OF HUNGER, THIRST, SEX

FIGURE 2–1.
Maslow's hierarchy.

sufficiently gratified their basic needs for safety, belongingness, love, respect, and self-esteem and are motivated primarily by trends to self-actualization. These characteristics are:[7]

1. Superior perception of reality.
2. Increased acceptance of self, of others, of nature.
3. Increased spontaneity.
4. Increase in problem-centering.
5. Increased detachment and desire for privacy.
6. Increased autonomy and resistance to the cultural mores and standards of society.
7. Greater freshness of appreciation and enrichment of emotional reaction.
8. Higher frequency of mystic experiences.
9. Increased identification with the human species.
10. Changed (the clinician would say improved) interpersonal relations.
11. More democratic character structure.
12. Greatly increased creativeness.
13. Certain changes in the value system.

Keep in mind, however, that this list of characteristics is based on Maslow's concept of "healthy people" and does not apply to his patients who, presumably, would have opposing characteristics. In other words, Maslow is describing people who have satisfied their basic needs.

Earl Kelley suggests the following characteristics of the "fully functioning self" (Maslow's "self-actualization").[8]

1. Fully functioning personalities think well of themselves.
2. They think well of others.
3. They therefore see their stake in others; that they and others are interdependent.
4. They see themselves as a part of a world in movement.
5. They see the value of mistakes.
6. They develop and hold human values; that is, values related to the welfare of people.
7. They know no other way of life except to keep within their values. They have no need for subterfuge or deceit.

8. Since their lives are ever-moving and ever-becoming, fully functioning people are cast in a creative role. They exult in being a part of the process of creation and in having an opportunity to facilitate it.

Carl Rogers offers some learning advice based on his broad experience in psychotherapy. We have paraphrased his "I" oriented findings to apply to "you" the reader.[9]

1. Be yourself. Do not pretend you are something you are not. Do not maintain a facade of false emotions.
2. Learn to listen acceptantly to yourself. Understand and accept your emotions. When "we thoroughly accept what we are, then change seems to come about almost unnoticed."
3. Try to understand another person.
4. Reduce communication barriers in other people.
5. Learn to accept another person. (This does not imply agreement with that person.)
6. Be aware of self and others and change will occur; you need not "[rush] in to fix things."

Rogers also advises:

1. Trust your own experiences. "If you feel it is valuable or worth doing, it is worth doing."
2. Evaluations by others should not be a guide for you. Listen attentively, but you must be your own evaluator.
3. Experience is the highest authority.
4. You should enjoy discovering order in experience.
5. Most people have a basically positive direction. They would rather build than destroy.
6. Life, at its best, is a flowing, changing process in which nothing is fixed.

We have discussed some of the characteristics of the self-actualizing or fully-functioning person and have briefly noted some of Carl Rogers's "learnings." Let us attempt, now, to suggest some positive attitudes and actions that the individual can adopt to become more self-actualizing. That is, what can you, the reader-communicator, do to more fully realize your potential; how can you attain a greater degree of self-actualization and become a more fully-functioning person.

Positive steps toward self-actualization

What can you, the individual, do regarding your own development? You can change if you wish. It depends a lot on your motivation. Do you really want to change? Are the rewards of a more complete, meaningful life worth the effort? Let us assume that you have all the motivation in the world—that you wish to start on a rigorous program of self-improvement. What do you do?

"Know thyself." This is an old adage attributed to Juvenal, the Roman poet. It seems to be a simple admonition, and yet you may discover that there are times when you do things that surprise you. You become a total stranger to yourself. One way to become better acquainted with yourself is to become more observant of the reactions of others to you. Watch for the nonverbal mannerisms in others that may indicate how they feel about you. If these reactions are negative, do something about it. Another way to learn about yourself is to be more introspective. Take time, perhaps once a week, to reflect on your actions of the recent past. Decide if you approve of those actions. If not, do something different the next time around. Also, there are various personality, aptitude, and other psychological tests available to you. Inquire about these at your student guidance office. *You* should be the expert on your personality.

Realize that you have hereditary and sociocultural traits. These traits have greatly influenced your development as an individual. Realize, too, that your sociocultural traits, though strong, can be modified. Truly, "a rose is a rose is a rose," and perhaps a leopard cannot change its spots, but you—a *Homo sapiens*—are neither a rose nor a leopard. You can change if you wish. Examine your values, attitudes, and beliefs. Do they meet the standards of logic? If not, do something about it. Change!

Try to better understand others. Listen carefully when your friends, associates, and co-workers talk to you. Avoid being abrupt, indifferent, or trifling as a listener. Instead, encourage others to express themselves fully and candidly. (See empathic listening in chapter 6.) Remember that understanding is the first step toward resolving conflict and attaining mutually beneficial goals.

Learn to trust others. Assume the best in people. Most people are basically honest and fair-minded. The bad apples are few in number. On the other hand, do not be gullible. Let your common sense be your guide.

Become involved in the life experience. But be selective. Elect to experience what you believe will be good for you, what will contribute to your personal development. Involvement means cooperating with others, and cooperation is vital—both to the individual and to society. When you cooperate, you are a part of something, you accept responsibility for that something. Get involved!

Welcome change and adapt to it. This is not a static world. Everything changes. Be aware that life itself is a process; it is continuous, everchanging. Do not be horrified by change, do not dwell on "the good old days." Move on to the next challenge.

Establish realistic goals or objectives for yourself. Do not lose sight of these goals. Don't get sidetracked. Remind yourself from time to time of your objectives. On the other hand, upgrade or alter your goals as you become more discerning, more mature.

Be persistent. Don't give up an idea or planned objective too easily. Some things take a little time. Be patient. Give it one more try.

> This above all, to thine ownself be true
> and it must follow, as the night the day,
> thou canst not then be false to any man.
> —Shakespeare, *Hamlet*

Projects

1. Complete the Personality Inventory following. We assume that you will be frank and honest.

2. Group yourselves in pairs, one person interviewing the other. The Personality Interview may be used as a basis for the interview. (See Appendix for suggested questions to the interviewee.) When the interview sheet has been completed, it should be turned in to the instructor. New pairs may be formed for the second round of interviews.

3. The class will form small groups of five or six students per group. Each group will discuss one or more of the following subjects and be prepared to report to the entire class.

   a. Discuss the effects of the sociocultural environment on the members of the group. (See p. 24) Do you agree with the poem by Dorothy Law Nolte? Can you give some examples from your own lives illustrating the concept of environmental effects on the individual? What can the individual do about environmental conditioning?

   b. Discuss the observable and unobservable aspects of personality. (See pp. 25–26) Give examples or demonstrate the observable aspects of personality. Can you add to the list? How does speech indicate personality) Which of the unobservable aspects of personality can be altered? What traits could be added to the list?

   c. Discuss values, attitudes, beliefs. (See pp. 26–27) What is the difference between values and attitudes? Give some original examples of each. Do you agree with the Steele-Redding classification? How many of their values does the group have? What values would you add?

   d. Maslow vs. Kelley vs. Rogers. (See pp. 30–33) Compare the three lists of these psychologists. To what extent are they similar? Attempt to combine the three in one unified list.

4. The class is seated in a large circle. The instructor acts as moderator on the subject "Positive steps toward self-actualization." Do you agree with the eight points? (See pp. 33–34) In what way could the individual items be realized or implemented? Should additional items be added to the list? Explain.

Worksheets

Name _____   Section _____

YOUR PERSONALITY INVENTORY

Directions: Grade each trait with a score of 1, 2, 3, 4, 5, or 6 where 1 is a very low score and 6 a very high score. Be frank and honest!

Trait	Explanation	Score
Cooperative	(helpful, considerate, group-minded)	
Courteous	(polite, cultured, well-mannered)	
Dependable	(reliable, prompt, trustworthy)	
Generous	(benevolent, liberal, unselfish)	
Just	(fair, unbiased, even-handed)	
Kind	(warm, compassionate, sympathetic)	
Peaceable	(gentle, reasonable, noncombative)	
Sociable	(likeable, convivial, a good mixer)	
	Sub-total	
Creative	(imaginative, original, inventive)	
Determined	(resolute, firm, strong-willed)	
Dynamic	(active, lively, exuberant)	
Efficient	(able, competent, careful)	
Informed	(knowledgeable, aware, cognizant)	
Optimistic	(cheerful, hopeful, expectant)	
Proud	(self-satisfied, dignified, unashamed)	
Self-reliant	(independent, confident, assured)	
	Sub-total	
	Grand Total	

Comments _____

Subject_____Interviewer_____Section_____

PERSONALITY INTERVIEW

Directions: Using the Personality Questionnaire in the Appendix, grade the subject on each trait as follows:1 = Poor, 2 = Fair, 3 = Good, 4 = Excellent.

Trait	Explanation	Score
Cooperative	(helpful, considerate, group-minded)	
Courteous	(polite, cultured, well-mannered)	
Dependable	(reliable, prompt, trustworthy)	
Generous	(benevolent, liberal, unselfish)	
Just	(fair, unbiased, even-handed)	
Kind	(warm, compassionate, sympathetic)	
Peaceable	(gentle, reasonable, noncombative)	
Sociable	(likeable, convivial, a good mixer)	
	Sub-total	
Creative	(imaginative, original, inventive)	
Determined	(resolute, firm, strong-willed)	
Dynamic	(active, lively, exuberant)	
Efficient	(able, competent, careful)	
Informed	(knowledgeable, aware, cognizant)	
Optimistic	(cheerful, hopeful, expectant)	
Proud	(self-satisfied, dignified, unashamed)	
Self-reliant	(independent, confident, assured)	
	Sub-total	
	Grand Total	

Note: Do *not* return this to interviewee; hand it in to your instructor instead.

ATTITUDE QUESTIONNAIRE

Directions: Please answer all questions below frankly and honestly using the following scoring method. If your answer is Definitely No, give yourself a score of 0; if your answer is No, give yourself a score of 1; if your answer is Probably No, give yourself a score of 2; if your answer is Probably Yes, give yourself a score of 3; if your answer is Yes, give yourself a score of 4; and if your answer is Definitely Yes, give yourself a score of 5. When the test is completed, add your scores and show the total.

1. Should abortion (during the first three months of pregnancy) be the decision of the expectant mother and her doctor?

2. Are you opposed to hunting as a sport?

3. Should the federal government supply free birth control devices?

4. Are you in favor of bussing to ensure integration of the schools?

5. Should the death penalty be outlawed for premeditated murder?

6. Would you favor a carefully controlled program of mercy-killing?

7. Are you in favor of strong federal gun control laws?

8. Should marijuana be legalized?

9. Are you opposed to a peace-time military draft?

10. Are you opposed to the physical punishment of school children by school authorities?

11. Should prostitution be legalized?

12. Should tax incentives be given to those who limit their families to two children?

13. Would you favor a law permitting all sexual practices among consenting adults?

14. Should a program of sex education be started in grade school?

_____

15. Should the federal government provide a complete medical care program?

_____

16. Are you in favor of the Equal Rights Amendment?

_____

17. Do you approve of interracial marriages?

_____

18. Are you in favor of a sizeable cut in military expenditures?

_____

19. Are you opposed to the censorship of pornographic materials?

_____

20. Should dress and grooming on the job or campus be a matter of personal preference?

_____

Total

Note: Qualify any of your answers here, if you wish.

_____

_____

Notes

1. Harold Lasswell, "The Structure and Formation of Communication in Society," From *The Communication of Ideas*, L. Bryson, ed., (New York: Harper and Row, 1948), p. 37.

2. James C. Coleman, *Personality Dynamics and Effective Behavior*, (Glenview, Illinois: Scott-Foresman, 1960), pp. 45 ff.

3. Coleman, *Personality Dynamics and Effective Behavior*, p. 76.

4. Edward O. Steele and Charles W. Redding, "The American Value System, Premises for Persuasion," *Western Speech* 26, Spring 1962, pp. 83–91.

5. Joseph Luft, *Group Processes: An Introduction to Group Dynamics*, (Palo Alto, Ca: National Press, 1963).

6. Abraham Maslow, *Motivation and Personality*, (New York: Harper and Row, 1954), pp. 80–92.

7. Maslow, *Toward A Psychology of Being*, 2nd ed., (New York: D. Van Nostrand Company, 1968), p. 26.

8. Earl C. Kelley, "The Fully Functioning Self," *Perceiving, Behaving, Becoming: A New Focus For Education*, (Washington, D. C.: Association for Curriculum Development, 1962), pp. 19–20. Reprinted by permission of the Association for Supervision and Curriculum Development and Earl C. Kelley. Copyright (c) 1962 by the Association for Supervision and Curriculum Development.

9. Carl Rogers, *On Becoming A Person*, (Boston: Houghton-Mifflin, 1961), pp. 167–186. Reprinted by permission of Houghton-Mifflin Co.

Suggested Readings

Horton, Paul B. and Chester L. Hunt, *Sociology*, (New York: McGraw-Hill, 1964).

This book is a clearly written text on basic concepts in sociology. It is authoritative and well-documented. Pages 49–139 are particularly useful for communication.

Keltner, John W., *Interpersonal Speech Communication*, (Belmont, Ca: Wadsworth, 1970).

See Chapter 3, "Who is Talking to Whom, The Many Faces of You," which discusses the various dimensions of the self.

Chapter 3

The Message: Language and Meaning

Performance Objectives

After studying chapter 3, you should be able to:

1. Define *spoken language.*
2. Explain *verbal and nonverbal symbols.*
3. List the four types of sentences and give an example of each.
4. Explain *clarity* and *appropriateness* as applied to language style.
5. List the six-part classification of nonverbal language and explain each classification.
6. List six specific examples of nonverbal language.
7. Give some of your own observations of paralanguage as used by your peers and associates.
8. Explain *non-identity, non-allness,* and *self-reflexiveness.*
9. Explain *indexing, dating, etc., quotes,* and *hyphen.*
10. Draw and explain Hayakawa's Ladder of Abstraction.

Photograph by Jerald W. Rogers.

COMMUNICATION AND LANGUAGE

Language. What a wonderful invention! What a great communication tool! We use language to get and give information, to announce our intentions, to explain what happened yesterday and what will happen tomorrow. We pass the time of day; we comment on the likelihood of rain. This small talk has a socializing effect. It binds people together into a social family

But what is language? It is a system of agreed upon symbols, either written or spoken, that represent real-life things, actions, and events. People use these symbols to communicate with one another. Here we are especially concerned with spoken language, which we define as a system of verbal and nonverbal symbols used to communicate thoughts and feelings. Nonverbal speech includes factors of speech such as pitch, rate, and loudness, while verbal speech refers to words only.

In one sense, language is naming things. Thus, we call the furry little creature that says *meow* a cat—C A T, cat. This combination of three sounds, [k], [æ], [t], when uttered orally in rapid sequence, results in the word or symbol *cat* that we in English speaking countries *agree* will "stand for" the furry little creature that says *meow*.

There is a certain sequence or order in language communication. first, there must be some internal or external stimulus, often of a sensory nature, which is followed by perception or recognition. Then, if there is adequate motivation, the perception is translated into a verbal concept and uttered orally. Let's apply this sequence to our example above. We see a furry little creature (stimulus). We recognize it as a you-know-what (perception). And, since we want (motivation) others to see the creature, we say, "See the cat!"

VERBAL LANGUAGE IN SPEECH COMMUNICATION

Our agreed-upon language consists of words and actions that serve as symbols for certain objects or events (referents) and other words that serve as modifiers or connectives, such as adjectives, adverbs, and prepositions. Single words can be used to communicate, for example, "Yes," or words can be joined together as a sentence to express a more complicated thought. In either case, it is hoped that the listener will understand what the speaker means. That is communication.

Let us assume that we will communicate using only complete sentences. We will define a sentence as a grammatically complete group of words that expresses a statement, question, strong feeling, or command. Thus, there are four kinds of sentences: delcarative, interrogative, exclamatory, and imperative.

1. A *declarative* sentence makes an assertion: "The library is closed today."
2. An *interrogative* sentence asks a question: "What is your attitude toward the Equal Rights Amendment?"
3. An *exclamatory* sentence expresses strong feelings: "She is impossible!"
4. An *imperative* sentence expresses a command: "Pay attention!"

Your purpose or intent in the communication situation will determine what type of sentence you will use. If you wish to give information, you will probably use a declarative sentence that states facts, opinions, or value judgments. If you wish to get information, you will probably use an interrogative sentence—you will question someone. If you wish to express strong feelings, you will probably use an exclamatory sentence. And, finally, if you wish to bring about some positive or negative action, you might try an imperative sentence—an order or command, such as, "Drive carefully!" In some instances, however, these sentence types are mixed; for example, "Hear my side of it, won't you please?" is both interrogative and imperative. And, in some cases, an interrogative sentence may be interpreted as a declarative sentence. For example, the question, "It's raining out, isn't it?" is, in effect, stating, "It is raining." In analyzing or responding to any sentence type, one should consider the intent or implication of the message rather than the form.

Language style

The verbal language of oral communication; that is, word choice (diction) and sentence structure (syntax), should meet the following requirements: (1) It should be clear and (2) it should be appropriate for the occasion and the listener(s). Let's examine these two factors.

First, *clarity*. A message should be easily understood. It should consist of carefully selected words that best communicate the intended idea; the sentence structure should be logical and to the point. In general, the best speech communication consists of fairly simple, unambiguous words and short simple sentences. Unusual words and long complex or compound sentences should be avoided. Jargon, cliches, and overly-technical language should also be avoided. Be clear! Get to the point! Be understood!

The language of the message should also be *appropriate* for the occasion and for the audience. In some situations, for example, an informal gathering of friends, you may have considerable leeway in your choice of language components. Slang words and jokes may be appropriate. But in another situation, such as a job interview, slang expressions should be avoided and jokes should probably be restricted. When in doubt, refrain! And, of course, the language of the message should be appropriate to the intellectual level of your audience. The age, education, and sociocultureal level of the listener should determine the language level used.

NONVERBAL LANGUAGE

What is the difference between a written message and spoken message? The written message may contain the same words as the spoken message but that is about the only thing the two have in common. In a written message, gone are the vocal characteristics of speech—loudness, pitch, rate, vocal quality, and inflections. Gone, too, are the gestures—the smile or frown, the animated posture, the wink, the hand on the listener's arm. Obviously, there is much more to speech communication than the words. In some instances, the nonverbal components of a communication may be more important than the verbal components. Mehrabian suggests that in a situation involving "social feelings," the verbal part of the message accounts for only 7 percent of the total impact on the listener while the nonverbal components account for 93 percent.[1] In other words, in social communication, how you say something may be much more important than what you say. Keep in mind that nonverbal language includes both body movement and nonverbal vocal communication. Table 3–1 may clarify this concept.

TABLE 3–1. Verbal-nonverbal chart.

	Vocal	*Nonvocal*
Verbal	Spoken word	Written word
Nonverbal	Loudness, pitch, quality, rate, vocal variety, pauses.	Gestures, facial expressions, body language, proxemics, eye contact, objects.

There are various classifications of nonverbal language, some of which use coined terms.*   We will use the following classifications:

1. Paralanguage
2. Body language
   a. Hand and arm gestures
   b. Body movement and posture
   c. Facial expression and eye movement
3. Action language
4. Tactile language
5. Object language
6. Proxemics

Before explaining these terms, it should be pointed out that the use of these nonverbal communication factors may be either intentional (for example, pointing) or unintentional (for example, blinking). In either case, the nonverbal factor communicates. It tells something about your intent, your attitude, your personality.

Our first classification is *paralanguage*, the nonverbal *oral* components of speech. This category includes all the nuances of vocalization, including loudness, pitch, rate, quality, and inflectional patterns. How you use these speech factors often indicates your intent or your attitude toward the listener. Sarcasm, for example, is achieved by manipulating the various speech factors.

---

*Paul Ekman and Wallace Friesen, in "The Repertoire of Nonverbal Behavior: Categories, Origins, Usage, and Coding" (*Semiotica I*, 1969, 49–98), use the terms *emblems, illustrators, affect displays, regulators,* and *adaptors* to name various forms of bodily movement. *Emblems* are nonverbal acts that can be directly translated into a word; for example, holding up two fingers in a V-sign signifies the word *victory,* or, more recently, *peace. Illustrators* are nonverbal acts that usually accompany verbal speech and serve to further describe or emphasize the message. For example, when speakers describe the height of a child they may not only give the height in feet and inches but may also demonstrate the approximate height with their hands. *Affect displays* are facial expressions that usually express emotion. A frown, for example, may express doubt or disagreement. *Affect displays* may be either intentional or unintentional. *Regulators* are nonverbal acts that tend to control the flow of conversation, such as nodding the head in agreement, shaking the head in disagreement, holding up the hand to stop the speaker from talking further, and so on. *Adaptors* are unintentional bodily movements that often reveal the personal feelings of a listener. For example, such movements as hand rubbing, foot-tapping, smoothing the hair or clothing, and so on, are adaptors that indicate the feelings of a listener.

Paralanguage may be more important than we realize. As good communicators, we should be more aware of the communicative potential of paralanguage. In many instances, how you say something is more meaningful than what you say.

Body language includes gestures of the hand and arms, body movement and posture, and facial expression and eye movement. Hand and arm gestures may be expressive, as when you are demonstrating the size of an object; indicative, as when you are pointing a finger at someone; symbolic, for example, supplicating with palms turned up and arms outstretched; emphatic, if you are brandishing a clenched fist.

Gestures often supplement speech. (Courtesy of New York University.)

Do you understand what is meant by gesturing? If not, describe (aloud) a *spiral staircase*. Now describe an *accordian*. You probably gestured as you spoke.

Body movements and posture includes such movements as hunching the shoulders, crossing the legs, leaning forward, nervous twitchings, and folding the arms. Posture involves the carriage of the body as a whole. Your posture, stance, and body movements are good indicators of your attitude toward the communication situation. "Don't wriggle in your pew!"

We are probably more aware of facial expressions as communicators than other body movements. Your smile, frown, wrinkled brow, or pursed lips reveal your mood or your reaction to the communication situation. The eyes, too, communicate. Whether you look a person in the eye, lower your eyes, blink, wink, or squint tells something about you. "The eyes are the windows of the soul."

In our category *actions*, we refer to overt actions other than bodily movements. The way you walk, the way you swing your arms, shake hands, or participate in physical activities reveals something about you. Are you graceful or awkward, energetic or lethargic? Do you try to talk and chew gum at the same time?

Some people seem to want to touch the person to whom they are speaking. Others draw away from personal contact. This is *tactile language*. The degree of intimacy between two people is probably an important factor in the degree of touching used. Also, cultural differences determine the degree of touching used in communication. For example, people from Arab countries are inclined to stand quite close and touch each other in a conversational situation, whereas people in Western countries such as ours are inclined to be more reserved and prefer more distance between each other.

Object language refers to any object relevant to the communication situation. The clothing one is wearing, eyeglasses, any visual aid used, are all part of object language. Certainly, objects communicate. It has been said that "a picture is worth a thousand words." Could be!

Proxemics has to do with the distance between communicators. It also involves one's concept of personal space. Again, cultural differences affect the desired distance separating communicators. According to anthropologist Edward T. Hall, communication distances in the United States are *intimate* (zero to eighteen inches), as between lovers or very close friends; *casual–personal* (one-and-a-half to four feet), as between friends; *social–consultative* (four to twelve feet), as between salesman and customer; and *public* (twelve to 100 feet), as in a public speaking situation.[2] Again, the degree of intimacy and the nature and purpose of the interpersonal relationship are the chief determinants of communication distance. Different cultural groups also maintain varying communication distances.

The next time you visit an office, note where the occupant (professor, stenographer, businessman) sits in relation to his visitors. Does the proxemics of the situation give you any clues about the occupant?

Although studies in nonverbal language are fairly recent, some interesting observations have been made.[3]

1. Fear or tension may be indicated by rapid movements, rapid speech, folding the arms, crossing the legs, or cigarette smoking.
2. Frustration may be revealed by rubbing the back of the neck, wringing the hands, and quick breathing.
3. Hand-clenching, nail-biting, and pencil-chewing may show anxiety and lack of confidence.
4. Nose-rubbing, rubbing the eyes, and covering the mouth with the hands are signs of rejection.
5. Happy, goal-oriented people have a light, rapid walk, while dejected, unmotivated people walk with dragging feet and drooping shoulders.
6. When a group of people walk together, the leader sets the pace.
7. Open hands, open arms, uncrossed legs, and unbuttoned coats appear to indicate open and positive personalities; whereas hidden hands, folded arms, crossed legs, and buttoned coats appear to indicate defensive and negative attitudes.
8. A deep resonant voice is considered a mark of poise; whereas a thin-voiced person is viewed as nervous or immature.
9. A happy woman is apt to wear a brightly colored dress.
10. Clothes often indicate what a person would like to be; on the other hand, the clothing one wears often reflects one's self-image.

William D. Brooks sums up the concept of action language nicely:

Whether it is the "locked ankles" (I'm not giving anything away!); the tapping of fingers, doodling, toe-tapping, or ball-point pen clicking (I'm bored and impatient); the smoothing and arranging of hair, smoothing of the dress, balancing a shoe half on and half off, or the gesture of touching the breast (courtship and flirtation); or erect posture, shoulders back, and "steepling" gesture (confidence)—action language is rich in the communication of intended and unintended messages. If we could develop skill in reading action language consciously—in verifying their meanings in a given encounter—we could possibly prevent some of the communication breakdowns and misunderstandings we experience day after day. We might also learn more about our own action language and the effect we have on others through our nonverbal communication.[4]

> Words and deeds are quite indifferent modes of the divine energy. Words are also actions, and actions are a kind of words.
>
> —Emerson

GENERAL SEMANTICS

Alfred Korzybski (1879–1950), a Polish-American engineer and educator, is considered the founder of the general semantics movement in the United States. Korzybski, author of *Science and Sanity: An Introduction to Non-Aristotelian Systems and General Semantics,* 1933, conducted a series of lectures based on his book in the late thirties and early forties. He was also the founder and director of the Institute for General Semantics, which publishes *ETC, A Review of General Semantics.* Korzybski's philosophy, though not entirely new, brought various non-Aristotelian principles together in one book and kindled considerable enthusiasm among some American educators, such as Wendel Johnson, Irving Lee, S. J. Hayakawa, and Anatole Rappaport.

What is general semantics?

General semantics is the study of human reaction to signs and symbols. It is concerned with all of human behavior as such behavior relates to language. Hayakawa adds the following definition to his explanation of semantics:

It is a comparative study of the kinds of responses people make to the symbols and signs around them. We may compare the semantic habits common among the prejudiced, the foolish, and the mentally ill with those found among people who are able to solve their prob-

lems successfully, so that, if we care, we may revise our own semantic habits for the better. In other words, general semantics is the
study of how not to be a damn fool.[5]

What are some of the problems that we have in relation to language? In the first place, we rely so heavily on language that we often
forget that words are not things, that they are only symbols that
represent things. Also, we tend to forget that our concept of a thing
called to mind by a word may not be the same to another person—
hence, a communication failure. Thirdly, our language is limited—
limited to those who understand English and limited by our practice of
using the same word, in many cases, to stand for many different things.
For example, the word *love* has ten or more meanings. We often must
depend upon context to indicate the meaning of a word. Finally, we
often confuse a fact statement (Jim was driving at a speed of sixty miles
per hour) with an opinion statement (Jim must be drunk) or with a judgment statement (Jim ought to be locked up).

In the following discussion we will show how general semantics can
be used to combat these language problems.

Principles of general semantics

Non-identity means that words symbolize things but are not those
things.[6] The word is not the object, the map is not the territory. This
seems obvious but, unfortunately, many people react to symbols
(words) as though the symbols were the things themselves. Symbol-
oriented Joe Doakes sneezes when he passes a display of artificial
flowers; Mary Jane "loses her cool" when she hears the word *pregnant;*
Billy turns pale when he hears the words *castor oil*. Words affect us much
more than we realize and we should be more aware of this phenomenon.

Non-allness means that it is impossible to know everything about
anything. A description of an object does not represent all of that object
but only a minute portion. When we report an observation we abstract
(draw out) certain details but omit many others. The car salesman says,
"And here is a nice, clean 1967 model." He does not tell us that it has
100,000 miles on the speedometer, that the engine is burned out, that
the tires are smooth, the brakes shot, and so on. But, even if he did tell
us these drawbacks, he would still omit most descriptive characteristics
of the car. When we report an observation we abstract certain details but
omit many others. Figure 3-1 illustrates Hayakawa's ideas on the
abstracting process.[7]

VIII	Wealth (A high level of abstracting.)
VII	Farm asset
VI	Livestock
V	Cows
IV	Cow
III	Bessie, the cow (Labeling—a low level of abstracting)
II	Human perception stage
I	The external, nonlinguistic cow with infinite characteristics

FIGURE 3–1.
Hayakawa's ladder of abstraction.

Note that III, Bessie the cow, is a fairly low level of abstracting, but as we proceed up the ladder we become more general until Bessie is referred to as wealth. Although there is a need for high-level abstracting, there are many instances where, for the sake of clarity, low-level abstracting is preferable. When in doubt, use low-level abstractions.

Self-reflexiveness means that we use language to talk about language. We make maps of maps, statements about statements, and evaluations of evaluations. There are weaknesses in this practice of using words to describe words. For example, we look up the word *precise* in our dictionary and one of the definitions is *exact*. We look up *exact* and one of the definitions is *precise*. We're back where we started.

Life is a process. Life is never static. We are not the same person today that we were yesterday, or one second ago, for that matter. This principle leads to the concept that even truth is tentative because all things change. What was "true" at one time may not be true today. For example, in 1400 A.D. it was believed that the earth was flat. *Truth is tentative* because it is abstracted by human beings. Information collected by our senses is often inaccurate and we must be aware of the possibility of error.

Individual differences is the principle that no two things are identical. Just because two or more people have something in common, for example, white skin or membership in the same church, it does not mean that they are identical. Every individual, every phenomenon, every happening is different—one of a kind.

General semantic recommendations

Come to grips with the identification problem. Go over some loaded words or expressions such as *bussing, homosexual, pervert, criminal, ex-con, jail bird, prostitute,* or *syphillis.* Do you have an emotional reaction to such words? If you do, remind yourself that they are only print marks on a paper and not the things they represent.

Be wary of hasty generalizations. Avoid such words as *always, absolute,* and *never.* "Never say 'never' " is an example of an over-generalization.

Get into the habit of distinguishing fact statements, opinion statements, judgmental statements. Note this dialogue: "They're not married, you know." "Well, he probably wouldn't marry her." "I don't blame him; she's so cheap-looking." Can you identify the three types of statements?

Delay your response to emotional statements. Count to ten before replying to such statements. This will usually prevent an emotional response from you. (However, if someone yells "Look out!" in a loud voice, you'd better duck.)

Use operational definitions, if possible, when defining a word. An operational definition describes the operation leading up to the word. Thus, a chocolate cake is defined operationally by giving the recipe for the cake. A similar helpful device is a functional definition that tells what the word does. For example, a *cultivator* is a piece of equipment used to plough a garden.

Use the following devices literally when appropriate; but use them mentally in all cases.

Indexing. To overcome the allness fault of saying, for example, "All women are poor drivers," think "woman$_1$ is not woman$_2$" Social security numbers, license tags, and so on, are examples of indexing.

Dating. Include dates in your thinking, since all things change. For example, "President Nixon$_{1970}$ said. . . ."

Quotes. Use quotation marks when a term is used in a special sense as in " 'Truth' changes."

Hyphens. Use hyphenated or compound words to show interdependency of terms. For example, "Pseudo-social scientists say our socioeconomic heritage is not a determinant of our success."

Nonsense questions

Although our language is quite flexible, there are some limitations to its use. Some words, for example, *why, how,* and *should,* may be used in such a way that their meanings become limitless—nonsensical. Questions such as "Why was I ever born?" and "How can I be popular?" illustrate confusing, unanswerable questions.

A *paradox* is a type of nonsense question (or statement) that is self-contradictory, for example, "Have you stopped beating your wife?" Such a question, though structurally sound, is nonsense and does not warrant an answer—except for fun and games.

Final thoughts on general semantics

Some of the concepts of general semantics seem too simple to discuss; that the word is not the thing for example. We all know that the word is not the thing, and yet many of us react to a word as though it were the thing itself. We might blush when we hear a vulgar expression; we might become ill when we hear the word *blood*. The entire thrust of general semantics is that we must realize the nature of language and its limitations. We should not become paranoid because of a word. The old childhood chant, "Sticks and stones may break my bones, but names will never hurt me," should be a truism, but, unfortunately, names do hurt—and hence, general semantics.

Following is a rather abbreviated list of concepts of general semantics:

1. Words in themselves have no meaning; meaning is in the minds of the communicators.
2. The word is not the thing; the map is not the territory. And we should not react to words and maps as if they were things or territories.
3. We can never describe *all* of anything. We always abstract.
4. We must be wary of the allness fault. We must be aware of exceptions—of individual differences.
5. Life is process—a continuous changing. We are not the same person now that we were yesterday.

Projects

1. Work in pairs. One person demonstrates to the other a certain type of nonverbal language, for example, a smile. The second person identifies the nonverbal type from the classification on p. 47. After five minutes, the roles are reversed.
2. One pair of students demonstrates the first project to the class.
3. Define the word *paradox*. Illustrate your definition.
4. The class will identify the general semantic principle or device that would apply or should be applied to each of the following statements:
    a. One never steps in the same river twice.
    b. You can't sleep on the word *bed*.
    c. Excitability is the quality of being excitable; excitable is that which is capable of being excited.
    d. All students are irresponsible.
    e. The United States is experiencing a serious depression.
    f. The variables in a one-to-one communication are a source, a receiver, and a message.
    g. Jane blushes when the word *love* is spoken.
    h. Before 1492, the world was flat.
    i. Have you stopped beating your wife? Answer yes or no!
    j. Can God make a rock so big that He can't lift it?

Notes

1. Albert Mehrabian, "Communication Without Words," *Psychology Today*, Sept. 1968, p. 53.
2. Edward T. Hall, *The Hidden Dimension*, (New York: Doubleday, 1966), p. 163.
3. Webb, Ralph Jr., *Interpersonal Speech Communication*, (Englewood Cliffs, N.J.: Prentice-Hall, 1975), pp. 77–94; and Fast, Julius, *Body Language*, (New York: M. Evans and Co., 1970), pp. 9–16.
4. William D. Brooks, *Speech Communication*, 2nd ed., (Dubuque: Wm. C. Brown Co. Publishers, 1974), p. 165. Reprinted by permission of Wm. C. Brown Co. Publishers.

5. S. I. Hayakawa, *Symbol, Status, and Personality* (New York: Harcourt, Brace, and World, 1958), p. 10.

6. Wendell Johnson, *People in Quandries,* (New York: Harper and Row, 1946), pp. 205–215.

7. S.I. Hayakawa, *Language in Thought and Action,* 2nd ed., (New York: Harcourt, Brace, and World, 1964), p. 179.

Suggested Readings

Fast, Julius, *Body Language,* (New York: M. Evans and Co., 1970).

A book on nonverbal communication written for popular consumption. Many concrete examples are used to illustrate the several types of body language.

Knapp, Mark L., *Nonverbal Communication in Human Interaction,* (New York: Holt, Rinehart and Winston, 1972).

An excellent summary of nonverbal communication. Well documented.

McCroskey, James C. and Lawrence R. Wheeless, *Introduction to Human Communication,* (Boston: Allyn and Bacon, 1976).

A well-written easy-to-read text on interpersonal communication. See chapter 10 for a discussion of nonverbal communication.

Mortensen, C. David, *Communication: The Study of Human Interaction,* (New York: McGraw-Hill, 1972).

See chapters 5 and 6 for a somewhat advanced discussion of verbal and nonverbal communication.

Photograph by Jerald W. Rogers.

Chapter 4

Delivering the Message: Pronunciation

After studying chapter 4, you should be able to:

1. Describe the production of speech sounds, including the energy source, vibrating body, resonators, and articulators.
2. Explain the phonetic alphabet and be able to give a word illustrating each phonetic symbol, for example [b] as in *boy*.
3. Explain the phonetic vowel chart, distinguishing between high and low vowels and between front and back vowels. Explain the nature of diphthongs.
4. Explain the factors determining standard pronunciation. Explain who determines standard pronunciations.
5. List the six types or causes of mispronunciations.
6. Demonstrate to the class the standard pronunciations and meanings of the words listed on pp. 69–70.
7. Complete the dictionary project on p. 75.
8. Complete the dictionary project on p. 76.

THE PRODUCTION OF SPEECH SOUNDS

To produce speech sounds we must have a *source of energy* (the exhaled breath), a *vibrating body* (the vocal folds, or the air column itself), *resonating cavities* (the mouth, throat, and nasal passages), and *articulators* (the tongue, lips, teeth, hard palate, soft palate, and jaw).

Source of energy. We take air into our lungs to supply our bodies with oxygen—this is inhalation. We then expel carbon dioxide and other waste materials from our lungs—exhalation. This total breathing process, called respiration, is necessary to sustain life. In addition, exhaled air is the *energy source* that produces speech sounds.

Vibrating body. When we exhale, the vocal folds, two folds of tissue located in the larynx or voice box, vibrate. This vibration produces *voiced* sounds. All of the vowel sounds and many of the consonants are voiced sounds. Some sounds, however, are produced without vocal fold vibration. The air column, of the throat and mouth is set into vibration when it is forced through a small aperture. The resulting sounds are called *voiceless* sounds. The voiceless sounds are *p, t, k, f, s, h, wh* (as in *which*), *th* (as in *thin*), sh (as in *show*), and *ch* (as in *chew*). All other sounds are voiced. When whispered all sounds may be said to be voiceless.

Resonators. After sounds are produced, they are modified by the resonating cavities (throat, mouth, and nasal passages) through which the air stream passes. The resonating cavities make the outgoing sound stronger or weaker, giving it a different quality. This produces different sounds. We can control this resonating effect by changing the size and shape of the resonating cavities. Thus, we open our mouths wide to say *Ah* but change the mouth shape and round the lips to say *Oh*.

Articulators. We can further modify the airstream with the articulators: the tongue, teeth, lips, hard palate, soft palate, and jaw. By positioning the articulators in a certain manner, for example, we produce a *p* sound; by changing the positioning of the articulators, we produce a *t* sound.

> In order to produce speech sounds, we must have a source of energy, a vibrating body, resonating cavities, and articulators.

PHONETICS

Phonetics is the science of speech sounds. The term is also used to describe a special set of symbols developed by the International Phonetic Association (IPA). In the IPA system, one symbol represents one speech sound. For example, the phonetic symbol [i] represents the vowel sounds in the words *beat*, *see*, and *believe*; [ɪ] represents the vowel sounds in such words as *it*, *been*, and *fear*. The IPA system uses alphabetical symbols to represent consonants, when possible. Thus, *b, d, f, g,* become the phonetic symbols [b], [d], [f], and [g] as the initial sounds of the words *boy, dog, foot,* and *good,* respectively. A few consonants and most vowels are represented by special phonetic symbols.

A knowledge of phonetics and the ability to write words phonetically will help you to become more aware of the subtle differences in word pronunciations. Also, there is a growing tendency on the part of dictionary publishers to use phonetic symbols in place of the old diacritic, or pronunciation, markings. One dictionary, Kenyon and Knott, *A Pronouncing Dictionary of American English,* uses phonetic symbols only (See Figure 4–1 for phonetic symbols and key words.)

Special phonetic symbols

The division of vowels into *front, middle,* and *back* refers to the position of the tongue in the mouth when they are pronounced. The vowel chart in Figure 4–1 is based on a left profile of the face. The vowels are also placed in the chart according to the vertical positioning of the tongue; that is, the tongue is humped high in the mouth to produce [i] and [u], low in the mouth to produce [a] and [a].

Many people do not use the vowel [a] in its vowel form but only as the first element of the diphthong [aɪ] as in *right.*

The r-like vowel [ɝ], as in *bird* is used in stressed syllables, whereas the r-like vowel [ɚ] is used in unstressed syllables. Thus, the word *murder* in General American speech—that spoken in the North and West—would be transcribed [ˈmɝˑdɚ]; [mɜdə] in Southern and Eastern speech. Likewise, the [ʌ] vowel is used in stressed syllables, while the schwa [ə] , the neutral vowel, as in *above,* is used in unstressed syllables. Thus, the word *above* would be transcribed phonetically as [əˈbʌv]

In phonetic transcriptions, the stress or accent mark in multisyllabic words *precedes* the stressed syllable, for example, [p ə' l i s] for *police.*

A working knowledge of phonetics will help you in your speech improvement program.

CONSONANTS

[p] pop	[b] bob	[t] tot	[d] dad	[k] kick
[g] gag	[s] sauce	[z] zoo	[f] fife	[v] view
[r] red	[l] lily	[w] we	[h] how	[m] mom
[n] nine	[ŋ] sing	[j] yet	[hw] which	[ʃ] show
[ʒ] pleasure	[θ] thin	[ð] then	[tʃ] church	[dʒ] judge

There are twenty-five consonant sounds.

VOWELS

Front Vowels		*Middle Vowels*		*Back Vowels*	
i	eat	ɝ	first	u	boot
ɪ	it	ɜ	first (Southern dialect)	ʊ	good
e	ate	ɚ	father	o	obey
ɛ	get	ʌ	cup (stressed)	ɔ	law
æ	cat	ə	above (unstressed)	ɒ	wash*
a	aunt*			ɑ	calm

*As pronounced by some people

DIPHTHONGS

eɪ	say	aɪ	right
oʊ	so	ɔɪ	boy
aʊ	out	ju	few

There are approximately twenty vowel (and diphthong) sounds.

FIGURE 4–1.
Phonetic symbols and key words.

DIAGNOSTIC MATERIALS: READINGS AND TOPICS

Directions: Read aloud the following materials. Use a loudness level adequate for the room size.

My name is _____. The social and economic value of good speech cannot be overestimated. But many college students are either unmindful of their faults or fail to realize that poor speech can hinder their chances of success in later life. They are unaware that mis-pronouncing such words and phrases as *singer, longer, English language, long ago,* and *bringing apples* is as serious a fault as is pronouncing *learn, earth,* and *thirty-third* as if they rhymed with *boy* and *rejoice.* They do not realize that the omission of sounds in such words as *didn't, couldn't, government, kept,* and *William* is an error that obstructs good communication. Consistent students, by giving careful attention to the laws of what might be called the science of speech, may reduce the number of their own mispronunciations and articulatory faults.

These heroes are dead. They died for liberty—they died for us. They are at rest. They sleep in the land they made free, under the flag they made stainless, under the solemn pines, the sad hemlocks, the tearful willows, and the embracing vines. They sleep beneath the shadows of the clouds, careless alike of the sunshine or storm, each in the windowless palace of rest. Earth may run red with other wars; they are at peace. In the midst of battle, in the roar of conflict, they found the serenity of death. I have one sentiment for the soldiers, living and dead—cheers for the living and tears for the dead.
—Robert Ingersoll, *Complete Lectures of Robert Ingersoll*

Impromptu topics

1. Population control in the United States.
2. The preservation of our natural resources.
3. What laws should be passed regarding the use of marijuana?
4. What policy should state governments adopt toward capital punishment?
5. What is happiness?

DIAGNOSTIC MATERIALS: ARTICULATION OF SPEECH SOUNDS

Directions: Read aloud those sentences designated by your instructor.

Consonants

1. Please bring your lab test papers to the
   desk.   p, b, t, d

2. Where can I get a good quality suit to
   wear?   hw, k, g, w
3. Both of the brothers were over fifty-five. θ, ð, v, f
4. Zelda's sister blushed with pleasure.   z, s, ʃ, ʒ
5. The judge charged Charles with running
   a red light.   dʒ, tʃ, r, l
6. No one knows the meaning of the Mona
   Lisa smile.   n, m
7. The lingering singers sang with all their
   strength.   ŋ
8. How do you know how young you are?   h, j

Vowels

9. If he is late today, he will miss his date.   ɪ, i, e
10. When Tom gets back, have him call
    Homer.   ɛ, ɑ, æ, o
11. Look at Luke; his foot is in the boot!   ʊ, u
12. The iron girder swung above the worker.   ɜ, ə, ɝ, ɚ, ʌ
13. Father parked his car on the lawn.   ɑ, ɔ

Diphthongs

14. Today is payday! Hurray!   eɪ
15. The answer is no—N O—NO!   oʊ
16. My kite is high in the sky.   aɪ
17. Roy gave a toy to the boy.   ɔɪ
18. Hugh was one of the few to be cured.   ju
19. How now, brown cow?   aʊ, ɑʊ

PRONUNCIATION

We have discussed the production of speech sounds. But sounds alone do not enable us to communicate; we must put the sounds together in words, phrases, and sentences to have a meaningful language. Pronunciation is the selection, production, and joining of individual speech sounds to produce recognizable word symbols.

Pronouncing a word

In order to pronounce a given word, we must know which sounds are required for the word and how to produce (articulate) those sounds correctly and in the proper sequence. Furthermore, with multisyllabic words, we must know which syllable should receive the emphasis or stress. Failure to observe these requirements may result in one or more of the following faults:

1. Individual sounds may be distorted to the extent that they become unacceptable as standard pronunciations.
2. An incorrect sound may be substituted for a desired sound. For example, *going* becomes *goin; this* becomes *dis.*
3. Sounds may be incorrectly transposed. For example, *pretty* becomes *perty; perspire* becomes *prespire.*
4. A required sound may be omitted. For example, *kept* becomes *kep; government* becomes *govment.*
5. An unrequired sound may be added. For example, *singer* becomes *singger; idea* becomes *idear.*
6. In multisyllabic words, the syllable stress or accent may be inappropriate.
   For example, *polICE* becomes *POlice; iDEa* becomes *Idea.*

Remember, ignorance of sound structure, faulty sound production, and unfamiliarity with proper syllable stress result in sound distortions, substitutions, transpositions, omissions, additions, and incorrect syllable stress—mispronunciation!

Who determines 'correct' pronunciation?

Many people think that dictionary publishers arbitrarily determine how words should be pronounced. This is not true. Dictionaries only record how words are being pronounced in educated circles in various parts of the country. Therefore, we might say that pronunciation standards are determined by the people, especially those educated people who more frequently use the spoken word.

It is probably unwise to consider pronunciation standards in terms of "correctness." Many words have two or more acceptable pronunciations and our language is always undergoing change. Today's pronunciation error may well become tomorrow's standard usage. A more realistic approach to pronunciation is to consider preferable those pronunciations that are in the widest use among the educated people of a given area in the country.

Regional variations in pronunciation

In the United States, there are three large areas that may be differentiated with regard to pronunciation habits. These are General American, which is used in the northern states, Eastern Standard, which is used in New York City, to some extent, and New England, and Southern, which includes the states south of the Mason–Dixon line. The standard pronunciations used in any of these three areas may be considered acceptable language.

> You should use those pronunciations and language customs that are standard in your area of the country.

SPEECH 'ON THE WING'

There is often a difference in the pronunciation of a word in isolation and the same word in a phrase or sentence. For example, pronounce the following words: *Monday, and, to.* You probably pronounced these words [m ʌ n d e ɪ], [æ nd], and (tu). Now speak the following sentence rapidly: "John and I went to town on Monday morning." If you spoke this sentence normally, you probably said, "John n I went tuh town on Mondi morning." Note that *and* becomes *n, to* becomes *tuh*, and *Monday* becomes *Mondi*. This is normal speech, speech on the wing. But often we fail to hear ourselves as we actually speak. We think that we pronounce words the same in context as we pronounce them in isolation. Not true! When speaking, it is customary to slight the unimportant words—the connectives, modifiers, and so on—and to stress the important words. In this process the sounds of the unimportant words are apt to be omitted or modified.

Read the following sentences aloud at a normal rate. Determine to what extent you modify the unimportant words but note the difference when you stress these words to achieve a particular meaning.

1. Give him his share of the money.
2. What do you think I said to him then?
3. I'll have an order of ham and eggs, please.
4. Mary and Ruth want to go with them in the car.
5. I go to class on Mondays, Wednesdays, and Fridays; I work on Tuesdays and Thursdays.

Improving poor pronunciation patterns

1. Get into the dictionary habit. Provide yourself with a good desk dictionary such as *Webster's New World Dictionary*, 2nd ed., (World Publishing Co.); *The Random House College Dictionary*, Revised ed., (Random House, Inc.); or *Webster's New Collegiate Dictionary*, 8th ed.,

Observe your mouth forming sounds. (Courtesy of New York University.)

(G. & C. Merriam Co.). When you hear or read an unfamiliar word, look it up in your dictionary. If this is inconvenient, jot down the word in a small notebook and consult your dictionary later. If two or more pronunciations are given for the same word, use the pronunciation that seems more natural to you. If the word is entirely unfamiliar, use the dictionary's first-listed pronunciation.

> A word of caution: dictionaries are not infallible. They do not determine standards of pronunciation; they only record pronunciations that appear to be current among educated speakers in various parts of the country.

2. Listen to the pronunciations and other speech habits of leading television and radio speakers. In general, the speech of such experts is good and should serve as a suitable model.
3. Keep a list of words that give you difficulty. Look up these words in your dictionary and practice using them correctly in everyday speech situations.
4. Be conscious of your speech. Many mispronunciations are caused by carelessness or laziness. A little effort and willpower will do wonders in any speech improvement program.

Projects

Mispronunciations are the result of sound distortions, substitutions transpositions, omissions, additions, and improper syllable stress. If you are guilty of some of these faults, and most of us are, it may be due to unfamiliarity with the correct pronunciation of certain words or, more commonly, carelessness or laziness in the production of speech sounds. No matter what the reasons are, your pronunciation habits can be improved by concentrated practice.

> To be an effective speaker, you must be easily understood and meet the pronunciation standards of your region of the country.

The following drills can be used to overcome careless habits of pronunciation. But before beginning the actual drills, here are a few general suggestions:

1. Practice in ten minute periods three or four times each day.
2. Use a mirror to see how you form individual sounds.
3. Begin the drills at a slow rate, exaggerating the sounds of each word. Gradually speed up to normal rate.
4. If possible, practice in a room where you will have privacy and freedom from interruption.

Drill 1: Distortions and substitutions

Study the following list of words and determine what pronunciation error could be made in each. Then read each word aloud, correctly. (If in doubt of the correct pronunciation, refer to your dictionary.) Your first reading should be at a very slow rate, exaggerating the production of each sound. Repeat this drill five times, gradually increasing your rate until each word is pronounced in a normal manner.

ten	down	that	college	chimney
men	town	this	language	pumpkin
said	Myrtle	cattle	mother	chasm
fail	first	little	father	gesture
dead	take	length	baseball	architect

head	naked	strength	Miss	sail
err	ham	singing	pity	genuine
bade	fine	going	direct	piano
oil	time	both	which	wrestle
boil	my	with	whale	deaf

Read the following sentences aloud. Be on guard for distortions and substitutions. Repeat each sentence five times.

1. Ten men worked at Earl Smith's Standard Oil Station.
2. Miss Myrtle Brown was taking singing lessons downtown.
3. The little girl liked to play the piano.
4. Take a language course when you go to college.
5. I threw the baseball with all my strength.

Drill 2: Transpositions

Follow the instructions for Drill 1.

ask	children	prevent	larynx
hundred	pretty	pharynx	perspiration
secretary	relevant	modern	introduce
cavalry	pattern	pretend	prepare

Read the following sentences aloud. Be on guard for transpositions. Repeat five times.

1. Ask the secretary to give you a hundred envelopes.
2. The larynx is the voice box; the pharynx is the throat.
3. Tanks are the modern equivalent of cavalry.
4. Introduce me to that pretty girl.
5. It is relevant that men perspire but modern women glow.

Drill 3: Omissions and additions

Follow the instructions for Drill 1.

kept	didn't	very	across
asked	company	fourteen	drowned
four	recognize	wouldn't	escape

door	particular	poem	idea of
gentlemen	government	distinct	athlete
diamond	William	told	go away

Read the following sentences aloud. Be on guard for omissions and additions. Repeat five times.

1. Ken Stringer was a valuable player because of his height.
2. The diamond didn't match the other fourteen jewels.
3. The airplanes attacked the column in the arctic.
4. Didn't you recognize the president in the government building?
5. William was drowned trying to escape.

Drill 4: Vowel recognition and syllable stress

1. Rearrange the words in Column 2 in the blanks provided so that the vowel sounds of Column 2 words match the vowel sounds of Column 1 words.

1		2
sleet	_____	said
bit	_____	loop
bet	_____	sale
bait	_____	him
bat	_____	oil
law	_____	town
cook	_____	dance
boot	_____	leap
girl	_____	calm
cup	_____	first

boy	_____	pull
out	_____	mine
light	_____	love

2. Underline the stressed syllables in the following words and, using phonetic symbols, write the vowel of each stressed syllable in the space provided.

refer	_____	income	_____	incomplete	_____
detail	_____	police	_____	retail	_____
data	_____	status	_____	legality	_____
idea	_____	perform	_____	romance	_____
industry	_____	except	_____	industrious	_____

Drill 5: Misplaced stress

Look up the pronunciation of the following words in your dictionary. Underline the stressed syllable in each word. Pronounce each word slowly and distinctly. Repeat five times.

acumen	museum	incognito	comparable
municipal	despicable	admirable	contribute
applicable	decade	cement	sepulchre
condolence	theater	police	lamentable
robust	preferable	formidable	hyperbole
hospitable	inclement	gondola	clandestine
grimace	secretive	impious	exigency
impotent	epitome	reputable	machination
amicable	detail	alias	romance
cabal	curtail	influence	debate

Drill 6: Tongue twisters

Although tongue twisters may be impractical for use in everyday speech situations, they do have value in articulation practice. Also, they're fun! Read the following tongue twisters slowly the first time, with exaggerated articulation of each sound; then read as rapidly as possible without missing a sound. Repeat each sentence five times.

1. A big black bug bit a big black bear, made the big black bear bleed.
2. Fanny finch fried five floundering fish for Francis Fowler's father.
3. Buy a pair of rubber baby buggy bumpers.
4. Amidst the mists and coldest frosts
   With barest wrists and stoutest boasts
   He thrusts his fists against the posts
   And still insists he sees the ghosts.
5. Silly Sally sells seashells by the sea shore.
6. The seething sea ceaseth, and thus the seething sea recedeth.
7. Around the rugged rock the ragged rascal ran.
8. Slippery sleds slide smoothly down the sluiceway.
9. Does this shop stock short socks with spots?
10. Theophilus Thistle, the thistle sifter, sifted a sieve of unsifted thistles. Where is the sieve of unsifted thistles Theophilus Thistle, the thistle sifter, sifted?

Worksheets

Name: _____

DICTIONARY PROJECTS

Drill 1: Dictionary analysis

Write your answers to the following questions in the spaces provided.

1. Give the name and date of publication of the dictionary you used for this project.

   _____

2. What are "diacritics?" How are they used? Give examples.

   _____

   _____

   _____

3. Where are the key words found? _____

4. If you cannot interpret a key word, on what page of your dictionary can you find more complete information? _____

5. On what pages can a general discussion of pronunciation be found?

   _____

6. Of what value can knowing the derivation of a word be to you?

   _____

7. Where is the accent placed to indicate primary stress? _____

   _____

8. How is secondary stress indicated? _____

9. Write the word *extraordinary* in diacritics, showing primary stress.

   _____

10. Write the word *challenge* in diacritics, showing primary stress.

   _____

Drill 2: Practice in dictionary usage and phonetic transcription

Complete the information called for by the column headings. Include primary stress marks *preceding the stressed syllable*. After completing each word, read the word aloud correctly.

Word	Phonetics	Meaning
1. acumen		
2. admirable		
3. alias		
4. arctic		
5. athletic		
6. bade		
7. burial		
8. cavalry		
9. columnist		
10. combatant		
11. comparable		
12. comptroller		
13. err		
14. film		
15. grievous		
16. grimace		
17. height		
18. impotent		
19. mischievous		
20 secretary		

Suggested Readings

Anderson, Virgil A., *Training the Speaking Voice*, 2nd ed., (New York: Oxford University Press, 1961). This book offers good treatment of speech production and voice theory. There are many reading selections dealing with voice improvement.

Fisher, Hilda B., *Improving Voice and Articulation*, 2nd ed., (Boston: Houghton-Mifflin Co., 1975). A carefully planned presentation of speech sound production, articulation, voice, and pronunciation, *Improving Voice and Articulation* provides many exercises for each sound.

Gorden, Morten J. and Helene W. Wong, *A Manual for Speech Improvement*, (Englewood Cliffs, N.J.: Prentice-Hall, 1961). This book is well organized. The text covers phonetics, the speech mechanism, voice, and contains numerous drills on vowels and consonants.

Gray, Giles W. and Claud M. Wise, *The Bases of Speech*, 4th ed., (New York: Harper and Row, 1959). This is a definitive text on the basic elements of speech. It is of special interest to the speech major.

Jones, Merritt and Mary Pettas, *Speech Improvement: A Practical Program*. (Bradenton, Florida: Communication Research Institute, 1974). *Speech Improvement* is a helpful text that covers articulation, pronunciation, voice, dictionary usage, and is replete with drill materials.

Leutenegger, Ralph R., *The Sounds of American English: An Introduction to Phonetics*, (Glenview, Illinois: Scott, Foresman & Co., 1963). This is a good introductory text for those studying speech improvement. It contains many phonetic drills, including a section of phonetic crossword puzzles.

Chapter 5

Delivery: Vocal Variety

Performance Objectives

After studying chapter 5, you should be able to:

1. Explain and demonstrate the function of loudness in speech communication.
2. Explain and demonstrate the function of pitch in speech communication.
3. Explain and demonstrate the function of rate in speech communication.
4. Explain and demonstrate the function of voice quality in speech communication.
5. Explain and demonstrate how emphasis or stress is achieved in speech communication.
6. Demonstrate your mastery of the above speech factors by reading to the class one or more of the selections on pp. 89–90.
7. Select an interesting reading of your own choice and read it to the class. Time limit—three minutes.

Photograph by Jerald W. Rogers.

Loudness, pitch, rate, and quality are the ingredients of vocal variety. You should develop the ability to vary these factors for purposes of emphasis and holding attention.

LOUDNESS OR INTENSITY

The loudness or intensity of your speech should always suit the occasion; that is, you should be easily heard by all your listeners at all times. Obviously, if you are speaking to many people in a large hall or room, you will have to increase the loudness level of your speech so that the people sitting in the back row can hear you. On the other hand, if you are speaking to only one person, your loudness level may be reduced.

Changes in loudness level may also be used for emphasis or stress. The important words of your spoken message may be stressed by increasing the loudness level on those words. Also, of course, a variety of loudness level will prevent monotonous delivery. Practice the following drills to check your loudness level and use of loudness variety.

Drill 1: To check loudness level

1. Read a short selection to a friend seated five feet from you. Have the friend grade you on loudness level as follows:
   Adequate _____   Too Loud _____   Too Soft _____
   Monotonous _____
2. Repeat this test at a distance of twenty feet.
3. Repeat the loudness test at a distance of forty feet. This distance would be equivalent to a large room or small auditorium.
4. Repeat the above tests using general conversation instead of reading. How were your scores?

Drill 2: Practice in loudness variation

Have a friend or member of your family listen to you as you read the following selection. Ask your audience to tell you if your overall loudness level is satisfactory; that is, if it is easily heard but not too loud for the situation. Use a *variety* of loudness levels.

They tell us, Sir, that we are weak; unable to cope with so formidable an adversary. But when shall we be stronger? Will it be the next week, or the next year? Will it be when we are totally disarmed, and when a British guard shall be stationed in every house? Shall we gather strength by irresolution and inaction? . . . Why stand we here idle? What is it that the gentlemen wish? . . . Is life so dear, or peace so sweet, as to be purchased at the price of chains and slavery? Forbid it, Almighty God! I know not what course others may take; but as for me, give me liberty or give me death!

—Patrick Henry, Speech to Virginia Convention

Use your voice to hold interest. (Courtesy of Adelphi University.)

PITCH

The pitch of your voice should be suitable for your sex and age. That is, if you are a male adult, the listener expects to hear a fairly low-pitched voice; if you are a female adult, the listener expects to hear a relatively higher-pitched voice. Children, of course, are expected to have higher pitched voices than adults.

Aside from the differences in pitch based on sex and age, there are two other aspects of pitch that should concern you: (1) your optimum pitch, which is the pitch that best suits your speech mechanism, and, hence can be produced with the greatest ease; and (2) your pitch variety, or your ability to vary your pitch to express different shades of meaning.

Your optimum pitch is usually the fourth or fifth note above the lowest note you can produce. Beginning with this lowest note, sing up the scale: *do, re, mi, fa, sol.* Now contrast *fa* and *sol.* The note that seems the easier to produce is probably your optimum pitch. Repeat this experiment using a piano, if one is available.

Your pitch should also be varied below and above your optimum pitch. Sing up the scale once again. Can you sing an octave (eight notes)? Two octaves (fifteen notes)? In everyday speech, you will probably want to use a pitch range varying from two to three notes below your optimum to four or five notes above your optimum.

Practice the following drills to improve your use of optimum pitch and pitch variety.

Drill 1: Practice in the use of optimum pitch

Using your optimum pitch, prolong the following vowels for approximately ten seconds each. Repeat this drill five times.

ah -------------------------------------- oh --------------------------------------

ee -------------------------------------- oo --------------------------------------

Using your optimum pitch only, read the following words and sentences. Note that reading sentences at one pitch is unnatural. This type of one-pitch speech is called a *monotone.*

speech	this	say	get
that	law	soft	boat
good	do	first	one
sound	right	joy	give

This is mine. Where are you? Give that to me, please. Did you see him?

Keep off the grass! No one told me a thing. Do you own a boat? What in the world happened to you? Yes, I agree.

Drill 2: Practice in use of pitch variety

A. Read the short sentences with the suggested pitch change on some words. This type of pitch change is called a *step*.

This is mine.   *Where* *are* you?   Give that to *me* please.

Did *you* *see* him?   *Keep off* the grass!   *No* one told *me* a *thing*.

Do *you* own a *boat*?   *What* in the *world* happened to you?

Yes, I a *gree*.

B. A pitch change on one syllable is called an *inflectional* change. Such a change could be upward, downward, or circumflex (upward and then downward). Read the following words with upward inflection, downward inflection, and no inflection. Do you capture the different meanings suggested in each case?

      Oh-------------------surprise, understanding, doubt
      Well ----------------waiting for an answer, disgust, doubt
      No ------------------surprise, disbelief, negation

Read the above words with circumflex inflection. What meaning does each word have now?

C. Read the following words and phrases, conveying the indicated meaning through pitch changes. In the third column, write the pitch change used: rising inflection, falling inflection, circumflex inflection, step change up or step change down.

Word or Phrase	Meaning	Pitch Change
now	Do you mean at once?	
now	At once!	
what	Sarcastic disagreement.	
hello	Who is it?	
oh, no	Resignation.	
not again	Disgust.	
one more time	With delight.	

D. Read the following sentences using maximum pitch variety:
   1. Ready for the next exercise: up, down; up, down; up, down; one, two, three, four; one, two, three, four; rest.
   2. The giant tree trembled, shuddered, and then came crashing down. The cry of "timber" could be heard in the distance.
   3. Every evening, the little old lady would call her brood: "Kitty, kitty, kitty, Come kitty, kitty, kitty."
   4. I live way up there—on the very top of the hill.
   5. You can't mean Johnnie! He hasn't been here for a year.
   6. Now you tell me when the work is practically finished.
   7. Hello up there. Anybody home?
   8. Count off! One, two, three, four! One, two, three, four!

> Pitch variety enhances meaning and holds the attention of your listener.

RATE

Your speaking rate is the average number of words you utter per minute. Therefore, if you speak 500 words in five minutes your average is 100 words per minute (w.p.m.). A good average rate for speech is 150 w.p.m. But this does not mean that you will speak at this rate all of the time. In some instances you may be speaking at a rate of 100 w.p.m.; in other instances at a rate of 200 w.p.m. But the average *overall* rate should be about 150 w.p.m. When reading aloud, your rate should be a little slower than 150 w.p.m.

There are two ways to vary speech rate: (1) by varying the duration of individual speech sounds and (2) by varying the length of the pauses between words, phrases, and sentences. Try to use both of these methods to achieve an ideal overall rate and a satisfactory rate variety within the overall rate. Proceed with the following drills to improve your speaking rate.

Drill 1: Determining your present speech rate

A. Using a watch with a second hand, read the following material aloud at what you consider to be a normal rate. At the end of one minute, stop reading. Count the number of words read. This is your word per minute rate for the selection.

Speech rate is influenced by the ideas being expressed, the number of listeners, the occasion, the size of the room, and the complexity of the message. Also, rate may vary to suit individual personalities. For example, one of President Franklin Roosevelt's "Fireside Chats" was delivered at an average rate of 120 w.p.m., whereas Walter Winchell, a newscaster of the same period, often averaged over 200 w.p.m. in his broadcasts. Generally, an overall average rate should be neither so rapid that the speaker cannot be understood nor so slow that the listeners become bored. An overall average rate should fall somewhere between 140 and 160 w.p.m. A rate within these limits should prove effective for most oral communication situations. At any given moment, however, speakers may vary considerably from their average rates. Such variations help to convey the intellectual and emotional ideas being expressed and to prevent monotony.

The above selection contains approximately 160 words. Your rate for this particular reading should be between 140 and 150 w.p.m. If you read the entire selection in less than one minute, your rate was probably too fast. Read the selection again at a slower rate.

B. Retest your reading rate with a longer selection. Read for three minutes, count the number of words read, and divide by three. This will give you your word per minute rate for a three minute selection. Does your rate fall within the recommended limits?

C. Record a one minute talk on your tape recorder. Play back the tape and count the number of words in your talk. If your rate was less than 140 w.p.m., perhaps you were speaking too slowly; if over 160 w.p.m., you were probably speaking too rapidly.

Drill 2: Developing a flexible rate

Read the following sentences aloud in the manner suggested by the sentence message. Indicate after each sentence whether it should have been read at a rapid, slow, or moderate rate.

1. There he goes! See him! Over there!   _____

2. The old man plodded wearily homeward.   _____

3. And in the home stretch, it's Blue Boy by a
   head.   _____

4. I understand that you have an apartment
   for rent.   _____

5. The plane zoomed over the trees and was
   out of sight.   _____

EMPHASIS

To convey intellectual and emotional meaning in speech, you must adequately emphasize or stress the important words or phrases in your spoken message. Emphasis is achieved with loudness, pitch, and rate variations. Practice the following drills to improve your use of emphasis.

Drill 1: Altering emphasis to change meaning

Read the following sentences, first with emphasis on the first word, then on the second word, third word, and so on. How does the change in emphasis change the meaning of each sentence?

1. That one is mine.
2. Do you think she's beautiful?
3. Where is Mary?
4. That is your duty.
5. Let me do that.

Drill 2: Determining emphasis

The following sentences are unpunctuated. Determine how each sentence should be read, according to its intellectual and emotional meaning, then mark off the sentence as follows: indicate a slight pause with one vertical mark; a longer pause with two vertical marks. Show word emphasis by underlining once for slightly stressed words, twice for more heavily stressed words:

Sample: And at the far turn ‖ it's Gold Bug ‖ by a length.

1. War pestilence famine all mean but one thing death.
2. As they listened the tolling bell seemed to echo their mournful thoughts.
3. The train screeched jarringly to a halt ten feet from the open drawbridge.
4. John Doe poor fellow is quoted almost as often as anonymous.
5. Without thought without money without plans he was riding the bus to nowhere.

QUALITY

Quality is the term used to describe the tonal characteristics of the voice. In a narrow sense, quality is the effect of the resonating cavities on the overtones of a given sound. For example, the exclamation *ah* has a different quality than the exclamation *oh*, thus allowing the ear to recognize two different sounds. In a broader sense, quality refers to the pleasantness or unpleasantness of a voice. Therefore, we say that John Doe's voice has a pleasant, charming, or warm quality; whereas James Smith's voice has a breathy, harsh, or nasal quality. In this sense, we may consider quality the overall characteristic of the voice, including loudness, pitch, and rate as well as the overtone pattern.

It is probably true that the voice reflects a person's personality, or at least reflects how a person feels at a given moment. Thus, a chronic fault finder will have a nagging or whining voice quality, a fearful person will sound frightened, a person who is physically exhausted will have a tired quality. However, if we are aware that undesirable pesonality characteristics or temporary emotional states are reflected in our voices, we can take steps to remedy the symptom; that is the voice quality, if not the underlying cause of the symptom. The following steps are recommended to improve your voice quality:

1. Listen objectively to a tape recording of your voice. Is your voice pleasant or unpleasant to your ear? Can you describe any undesirable features of your voice, for example, is it nasal, harsh, breathy, thin, grating, hoarse, or whiney? Can you attribute any of the undesirable characteristics to a misuse of loudness, pitch, or rate? For example, is

your voice too loud or too soft; too high or too low; too rapid or too slow; or lacking in vocal variety?

2. Using the previous analysis of your voice as a guide, record additional material from any of the chapter selections. Concentrate on one speech factor at a time.

   a. Realize that good speech and good voice quality require physical effort and concentration. Don't be lazy! Don't be careless!

   b. Before reading, try to relax the throat muscles. Gently massage your throat. Rotate your head in a circular pattern to stretch your throat muscles. Open your mouth wide and yawn. Such preliminary exercises should make you aware of any undue tension in your throat musculature and help you to relax.

   c. Make sure that you have an adequate breath supply and that your breath is expended gradually and evenly in the production of clear tones in the breath groups of your reading.

Projects

Directions: Read the selection silently for meaning. Use your dictionary to check the pronunciation of unfamiliar words. Then read the selection aloud using maximum variety of loudness, pitch, and rate.

You come to us and tell us that the great cities are in favor of the gold standard; we reply that the great cities rest upon our broad and fertile prairies. Burn down your cities and leave our farms, and your cities will spring up again as if by magic; but destroy our farms and the grass will grow in the streets of every city in the country.

—William Jennings Bryan, *The Cross of Gold*

Sir, before God, I believe the hour has come. My judgment approves this measure, and my whole heart is in it. All that I have, and all that I am, and all that I hope in this life, I am now ready here to stake upon it; and I leave off as I began, that live or die, survive or perish, I am for the Declaration. It is my living sentiment, and, by the blessing of God, it shall be my dying sentiment; independence now and independence forever.

—John Adams, *Speech*

Not hear it?—yes, I hear it, and *have* heard it, long—long—long— many minutes, many hours, many days, have I heard it—yet I dared not—oh pity me, miserable wretch that I am—I *dared* not—I dared not speak! We have put her living in the tomb.

—Edgar Allan Poe, *The Fall of the House of Usher*

> Words always will get even: you may think
> that you are master of this regiment,
> each member stamped with clear official ink
> and guaranteed to go where it is sent.
> Such bending to your will is a mirage,
> for words have ways of making you half-blind
> while working out their schemes of sabotage
> against the manufacture of your mind.
> They seize upon the code-book of your heart,
> scanning the secret blueprints of your soul,
> then twist your rich experience apart
> and publish one poor fragment as the whole.
> Each time words gaze with meekness in your eyes
> you know they are destroying you with lies.
>
> —Harold Raymond Ross, *Sonnet**

*Reprinted by permission of Harold Raymond Ross.

I am the printing-press, born of the mother earth. My heart is of steel, my limbs are of iron, and my fingers are of brass. I sing the songs of the world, the oratorios of history, the symphonies of all time. I am the voice of today, the herald of to-morrow. I weave into the warp of the past the woof of the future. I tell the stories of peace and war alike.

I make the human heart beat with passion or tenderness. I stir the pulse of nations, and make brave men do better deeds, and soldiers die. . . . I am the laughter and tears of the world, and I shall never die until all things return to the immutable dust.

I am the printing-press.

—R. H. Davis, *I Am the Printing-Press*

Suggested Readings

Campbell, Paul N., *Oral Interpretation*, (New York: The Macmillan Co., 1966).

The author gives practical advice on the analysis and oral presentation of literature. See especially, Chapter 4, "Practice."

Eisenson, Jon and Paul H. Boase, *Basic Speech*, 2nd ed., (New York: The Macmillan Co., 1964).

This book includes basic materials on speech production, phonetics, voice, and diction as well as chapters on conversation, discussion, oral reading, and public speaking. See especially, Chapter 6, "Improving Your Voice" and Chapter 18, "Reading Aloud."

McCabe, Bernard P. Jr., *Communicative Voice and Articulation*, (Boston: Holbrook Press, 1970).

The greater part of this text is concerned with speech sound articulation. Part Two, Chapter 2, "Voice" deals with the factors of voice, briefly explains the factors and gives some drills.

Chapter 6

Hearing and Listening

Photograph by Jerald W. Rogers.

>

Listening is sometimes confused with *hearing*. Although there is a relationship between the two terms, they are not synonymous. Hearing is the perception of sound either consciously or unconsciously; listening implies the conscious attention to sounds for the purpose of identification or understanding. We may *hear* a sound without consciously listening for that sound. For example, we *hear* traffic noises, the chirping of birds, footsteps, or the voices of children playing outside our window but we are not consciously aware of these sounds because we may be listening (paying attention) to a television program.

In this chapter, you will be introduced to *listening* as an important aspect of oral communication. But, since listening implies an expectation of hearing sounds, you should have some knowledge of the mechanics of hearing.

HOW SOUNDS ARE PRODUCED AND HEARD

If you pluck a guitar string, the string vibrates back and forth causing a disturbance in the air. This disturbance travels through the air as a wave. Anyone within hearing range of this wave inteprets it as sound. In Figure 6–1 we examine the important factors in sound production.

The guitar string is at rest in position A, the solid line in Figure 6–1. When the string is plucked, it vibrates back and forth, first to B and back again through the starting point to C, and then back to A and so on. This completed double vibration, from A to B to C and back to A is called a *cycle*, or *oscillation*. The number of cycles that occur per second is called the *frequency*. Frequency is interpreted by the ear as *pitch*. The frequency of a vibrating body, for example, a guitar string, is determined by the length, diameter, and tautness of the string. A short string produces a higher pitch than a long string. A fine string produces a higher pitch

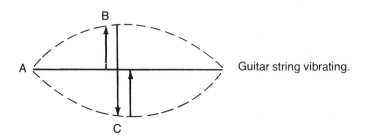

Guitar string vibrating.

FIGURE 6–1.
Guitar string vibrating.

than a heavy string. A tight string produces a higher pitch than a loose string. A guitar string of the proper length, mass, and tension will vibrate, when plucked, at a frequency of 256 cycles per second—a pitch of middle C.

The distance the string travels from A to B is called the *amplitude*. The greater the amplitude, the greater the intensity or loudness of the sound. The *quality* of sound is determined by the size and shape of the *resonating cavities* of the sound-producing instrument, for example the size and shape of the guitar body or the mouth and throat in the case of human speech. Quality enables us to distinguish one musical instrument from another or one voice from another.

When sounds are produced by a vibrating body, sound waves are sent out into the air in all directions. These waves travel through air at the relatively slow speed of about 1100 feet per second and gradually diminish in intensity or strength in proportion to the distance traveled. If someone is within hearing range of these sound waves, the waves will strike the person's eardrums and cause them to vibrate back and forth with the vibrating characteristics of the sound source. The eardrum vibration is carried mechanically by tiny bones in the middle ear (the malleus, incus, and stapes) to the inner ear (cochlea), where the vibrations are translated to nerve impulses and carried to the brain, which identifies them as sound. The characteristics of the sound-producing vibration, such as the frequency of vibration, the amplitude of the vibrating body's oscillation, and the effect of the resonating cavities on the produced sound, are interpreted by the brain as pitch, loudness, and quality, all of which will vary according to changes in the vibrating pattern of the sound source. Thus, the individual hearing the sounds will recognize changes in pitch, loudness and quality if the characteristics of the vibrations are altered.

There are obviously certain limiting factors in the hearing process. The sound source must not be too distant from the listener; the intensity (loudness) of the sound must be strong enough to be audible; and the frequency of the sound (pitch) must be within the audible pitch range of the ear. Human beings have an estimated audio pitch range from about 15 cycles per second to 15,000 cycles per second. Frequencies below and above these are inaudible to most human beings.

This brief description of the hearing process, although oversimplified, will give you a general concept of the mechanics of hearing and an awareness of the physical factors limiting hearing.

The act of *listening*, or of being consciously aware of sound for the purpose of identification or interpretation is different from *hearing*. We inadvertently hear an unusual sound. We say, "Listen! Wasn't that thunder?" Everyone present pays attention, concentrates, listens. The sound repeats itself. Yes, that was thunder.

We listen in order to identify or interpret the various sounds in our environment. But, although it is often important to be able to identify and interpret sounds, we are especially concerned, in this text, with the listening involved in oral communication.

THE COMMUNICATIVE ASPECT OF LISTENING

Throughout this book we have referred to "speech communication," but perhaps we should be more inclusive and make it "speech and listening communication." Certainly, we cannot communicate unless we have a receiver.

Reasons for listening to spoken messages

Why do you listen? Why should you listen? In some cases, you listen because your attention is captured. Someone shouts, "Look out!" Your attention is captured and you listen, perhaps in self-preservation. Or, the chairperson of a meeting you are attending bangs the gavel. Again you listen—perhaps out of curiosity or because it is the polite thing to do. Or, the loudspeaker on the Navy ship booms, "Now hear this!" Your attention is captured and you listen to the message that follows. All of the above are examples of *primary attention*. You are attracted by a loud noise or an unusual stimulus and compelled to listen, at least for a few seconds.

But now, why should you listen? If you listen "because you want to," it is called *secondary attention:* the reasons do not include the immediate stimulus of loudness or other unusual presentations. Your motivation to listen "because you want to" would be the result of self-interest, curiosity, entertainment, cultural conditioning, group interest, or altruism.

Self-interest is the strongest motivation to listen. You want to live; you have needs, appetites, desires to satisfy; you feel that you must better yourself, expand your horizons, be happy (a rather elusive goal). And so you listen to information, advice, warnings; to anything, in fact, that might be to your self-interest, as you see your self-interest.

Other motivations to listen are because your curiosity is provoked or because what is being communicated is funny or interesting—entertaining. The stand-up comedian makes you laugh, and you like to laugh; the teller of an off-color story excites you; explorers kindle your imagination with their descriptions of their adventures in the Andes. Entertainment is a fairly strong motivation to listen. Look at the popularity of television.

You also listen—attentively or not so attentively—because you have been conditioned to listen, especially to your elders. This is cultural conditioning. The teacher tells you to "pay attention"; you are *supposed* to listen to the sermon; you have been taught that it is polite to listen (and so it is). Although this is not the best motivation for listening, who

Listening to gain information. (Courtesy of Adelphi University.)

knows—sometimes you may hit pay-dirt and find that you are interested in what is being said.

Another motivation to listen is because you are group-minded. You want to help the group—including yourself. This type of motivation would be found in problem-solving discussion groups. You are a member of the group and listen to better understand and resolve a common problem. Commendable!

Sometimes you may listen to another person because you want to help that person. This is altruism. Your fellow communicator has a problem. Perhaps he only needs a sympathetic ear or a shoulder to lean on. Or perhaps you can give advice or suggest a remedy. Three cheers for this kind of motivation.

Now let us consider listening from a different point of view—for *understanding,* whatever the *basic* motivation for listening.

LISTENING FOR UNDERSTANDING

Most of us are poor listeners. We listen to a person for a few seconds and then our mind wanders. We think of a dozen things—what we are going to have for lunch, the letter that we didn't write, the news program of the night before, the girl in the front row—anything except what the speaker is saying. And yet, the speaker, whether a lecturer, a discussion panelist, our boss, or even a casual conversationalist, might be saying something of great importance to our well-being. How many times have we asked road directions from a filling station attendant only to forget half of the directions ten minutes later. "Did he say turn at the second light or the third?" Truth is, we didn't listen carefully.

Other communication problems may turn our attention away from speakers. They may have an unusual mannerism, speech habit, or gesture that we find distracting. Perhaps the speakers are difficult to hear or understand. Or we may disagree with their points of view and "turn them off" as we would a radio program. Or, we may be physically uncomfortable. Perhaps the seat is too hard, or the room is too warm or too cold.

If you are guilty of any of these poor listening habits (and most of us are), what can you do about it? How can you overcome the tendency to daydream or become sidetracked by other stimuli when you should be paying attention? Some common sense suggestions are as follows:

1. Realize that attention takes conscious effort. Make the effort to listen carefully. Exercise some will-power.

2. Realize that you may be missing something vitally important by not paying attention.

3. Be aware that attention to a speaker is a matter of common courtesy. When you speak, you will expect attention. Give that same courtesy when you are the listener.

4. Do not allow yourself to become distracted by anything unusual in the speaker's manner, speech, or dress. Eccentricities should not hinder the reception of a worthwhile message.

5. Concentrate on the main ideas expressed. Disregard the non-essential, the redundant, the superfluous. Go over the main ideas in your mind. If convenient, jot down essential information that you cannot trust to memory.

6. If possible, try to control the physical factors of the listening situation. Switch off the television set, the vacuum cleaner, the gasoline lawnmower. Sit up front in the classroom, lecture hall, or auditorium for maximum listening comfort.

'Listening' with your eyes

Although we have already discussed nonverbal communication, including body language, in chapter 3, it is an important part of learning good listening habits.

You listen with your ears and, in most cases, "listen", see, and comprehend with your eyes. Don't minimize this important message receiver. Learn to use your eyes to interpret subtle shades of meaning or emotional overtones in the speaker's message or the listener's reactions.

You are having dinner with a friend and he is describing a misunderstanding that he had with a salesgirl about a credit card. Your friend, toying with his fork, does not look at you, but does glance over your shoulder as though expecting someone. Occasionally, he glances at his watch. Occasionally he loses his train of thought. Get the picture? What is the trouble here? What do you do—slip away into the night? Or stick it out?

A couple is eating breakfast. The man is reading the morning paper. The woman says, "What are your plans for lunch today?" The man mutters something unintelligible and raises the paper a few inches, hiding his face from view. What is your assessment of this situation? Is this a couple on their honeymoon? How long have they been living together?

Was the woman rude in interrupting the man when he was reading? Was he rude to read at the breakfast table? Does the woman get an answer to her question? What is the "visible" message to you, the invisible spectator.

These two examples illustrate the importance of visible communication. So, whether you are the source or the receiver, get into the habit of "listening" with your eyes. Keep your eyes on the other communicator. Watch for the frown, the smile, the nod, the shifting of weight on the feet, scratching of the head (or other parts of the body), shifty eyes, and so on. All of these visible signals will tell you a lot about other communicators: what they are thinking, feeling, and really want to say.

EMPATHIC LISTENING

A freshman signed up for a course in public speaking. His first few speeches were disastrous—he blushed, his knees knocked together (or seemed to), his hands trembled, his voice quavered, and he perspired profusely—a classic example of stage-fright. And the instructor, a grimfaced, older man, was of little help. He seldom looked at the

student, but busied himself, instead, with note-taking. And then things changed. The instructor, due to illness, was replaced by a friendly young man in his late twenties. Our frightened young student was again on the platform to go through his weekly ordeal. He clutched the edges of the lectern, gave his opening "attention-getter" and, finally, with considerable fear, looked up at the emotionless, indifferent, stolid faces of the audience. And then the student saw the new instructor in the back row. He was smiling, friendly. He nodded his head in approval as though he were saying, "Go ahead, you're doing just fine!" The student seemed to get the message. His voice became firmer, he became more relaxed, and he somehow forgot to be nervous. He finished his talk as he had planned it and even got a round of applause from his fellow students. After this startling but successful speaking experience, our student had no more stage-fright. Sometime later, he confided in us what he had felt on that memorable day: "I was pretty scared when I looked up at the bored faces in the class. Then I spotted the Prof. He seemed very friendly and helpful. He was smiling like he was my best friend and he kept nodding his head, 'yes, yes, yes'—to go ahead with my talk. And I did. Everything was alright. I even got a good hand from the class."

The above example may be a bit melodramatic, but it happened. And it points up the concept of empathic listening. The instructor was a friendly, kind human being. He sympathized with, understood, and encouraged the young student; he listened empathically.

Empathic listening, sometimes called noncritical or active listening, means that fellow communicators not only want to *hear* your message, but that they also want to know you as a fellow human being. They

want to tune in to your values, your feelings, your mood. They want, somehow, to be *involved* as a friend in the rather personal, self-revealing process of *your* communication. As John Stewart states in *Bridges, Not Walls,* "The goal of empathic listening is to *really hear the other person,* to begin to see things as he sees them, rather than looking at what he's saying only from your own point of view. Empathic listening is listening *with* instead of listening *to* another person."[1]

Empathic listening does not mean, however, that you do not evaluate the content of the message. It *does* mean that you hold back any evaluative or critical response until you truly understand the nature and essence of the *human* communication to which you are listening. There is no reason why empathic listening and critical listening cannot be practiced simultaneously in most communication situations. Here's an example. A friend of yours states: "I think we ought to drop a bomb on Upper Slobovia and wipe them off the map!" You want to reply, "How stupid can you be? That's the most ridiculous thing I ever heard!" Instead, you smile encouragingly and say, "I take it that you don't think much of Upper Slobovia."

Listening empathically does not mean that you agree with the speakers; it does not mean that you disagree with the speakers. It *does* mean that you try to see the issue from their point of view; that you *empathize* with their feelings; that you encourage them to express themselves fully. And *then* you reply!

Here is a suggested set of rules for empathic listening.

1. Realize that people are all individuals with their own values, feelings, and experiences.
2. Listen attentively to your fellow communicators. Try to see their points of view; try to sense their values.
3. Encourage them to express themselves fully.
4. Then, when you feel that you truly understand the communicators' points of view, paraphrase their concepts to their satisfaction.
5. Only then do you speak up for yourself!

> Try empathic listening at the earliest opportunity. You may be surprised at the results.

LISTENING FOR CRITICAL EVALUATION

There is also a place for critical listening, for reasoned evaluation in communication. In today's world, we are constantly bombarded with persuasion. "Buy this product!" "Vote for this candidate!" "Accept this doctrine!" "Do this!" "Don't do that!" The day doesn't go by that we are not required to make an evaluation, a judgment, a decision. With this in mind, it is easy to see that we should develop a critical ear to this barrage of education, propaganda, and super-salesmanship.

Isms Indeed

Ology this and ology that,
Isms and ists indeed.
Now it's the custom of each and all
To have a formidable creed.
A credo to swear by, a sage to quote,
And surely a flaming cause.
It must be so, the disciple says
And shows you his book of laws.
He argues the question pro and con,
Refers to Plato and Hume.
If you're not convinced of the truth, he says,
The answer to life is doom.
So, beware ye unbelievers,
And listen well—
The reward is heaven!
Otherwise, hell!

—M. B. Jones

What can you, the listener, do to become a more critical, evaluative judge of persuasive communication?

EVALUATING PERSUASION

Preliminary preparation

1. Become as well informed as possible on the important and vital questions of the day. Read books, magazines, daily newspapers; tune-in a daily television news program for up-to-the-minute newscasts and watch important documentaries furnished by the networks and educational stations. Keep up to date on the events in your community, your state, your world.

2. Check the source of the persuasion. If you read books, magazine articles, attend lectures, find out everything you can about the sources; that is, the authors or speakers. Are the speakers qualified by education and experience to discourse on the subject? How do they make

their living? Who employs them? What are their backgrounds? What do they have to gain by supporting a particular point of view? It may be difficult to find information on a persuader. Here are some suggestions:

a. Check *Who's Who in America, Dictionary of National Biograhy, Living Authors* and similar volumes.

b. Check the library card catalogue and the *Reader's Guide to Periodical Literature* for any writings by the persuader. Looking over such materials should help you to know the persuader.

c. Inquire among educators and others in the persuader's field. They may be able to give you valuable background information.

Analyzing the persuasive message itself

As you read or listen to persuasive messages try to answer the following questions:

1. What are the persuaders' specific purposes? What do they want you to believe or do?

2. What issues are involved? What are the main points of contention? Are there problems? Do the persuaders have solutions? Are the solutions practical? Do the advantages outweigh the disadvantages?

3. Are the persuaders' contentions supported by sufficient evidence? That is, do the persuaders offer proof to support their contentions, proof in the form of documented facts and expert opinion?

Your reaction to a speech

After carefully listening to a speech, you should come to one of three conclusions regarding the talk:

1. The arguments appear to be sound and adequately supported with evidence. The proposition is acceptable.

2. There were too many fallacies of evidence and logic. Unacceptable.

3. Some fallacies. Unacceptable until further investigation.

> To be a critical listener, you must keep informed, listen attentively, and understand the nature of evidence and reasoning.

Projects

1. The instructor selects five students to participate in the Gossip Chain. Students 1 and 2 step out into the hall or adjoining room. Student #1 reads, slowly and clearly, one of the messages below to Student #2, who listens carefully but does not take any notes. At the end of the reading, Student #1 returns to the classroom and Student #3 joins #2 in the hall. Student #2 will now *tell* #3 the message read to him. Likewise, Student #3 will tell the message to #4, and #4 will tell the message to #5. Then #5 will return to the classroom and tell the message to the class. The original message will then be read to the class and compared to #5's version. If time permits, other groups may be selected to repeat the experiment using the other "gossip messages."

   The purpose of this experiment is to demonstrate to the class how messages become distorted when passed on by word of mouth.

Sample gossip messages

There was a wealthy banker named Whiteside who lived in Austin, Texas. Mr. Whiteside wanted to buy a Ferrari to impress his friends. The banker agreed to purchase the Ferrari for a mere $12,000 from Bob Smith, the local dealer. Unfortunately, the car was not ready for delivery for six months and when it finally arrived, Mr. Whiteside refused to pay for it. Bob Smith sued Mr. Whiteside but they eventually settled out of court for a small sum. Smith's brother-in-law finally brought the Ferrari from the dealer for $10,000.

Please give my secretary, Miss Dowdy, the following message: Tell her that Mr. Rogers had to go to a convention in New York City. I'm leaving today, Wednesday, and I'll be staying at the Statler-Hilton Hotel. She can reach me there anytime Thursday, Friday, or Saturday. I'll be catching a return flight Saturday night at nine and I'll be in the office on Monday morning.

Also, have her cancel my Kiwanis meeting on Friday night. And tell her to complete the inventory on the Bantam Books and send the summary to the Vice President.

One more thing, be sure to tell her to feed the goldfish.

A young man named Albert liked to play pool but, since Albert was quite short, he was unable to play on a standard pooltable. He therefore decided to order a custom-built pooltable from a local manufacturer. He gave the order to a Mr. Jacobs, the manufacturer's representative. This table was to be two feet high and covered with an expensive leopard skin. The table was finally completed, but Albert decided that he wanted the table to have only one pocket instead of six. Mr. Jacobs had the table rebuilt at considerable expense and called Albert by phone. Albert now decided to have the table built with a slope running down to the single pocket. The change was made, again at considerable expense. When it was finally completed, the pooltable was delivered to Albert's residence but lo and behold, Albert had left town, with no forwarding address.

So if you know anybody who wants to buy a $10,000 pool table that is two feet high, covered with leopard skin, and slopes down to a single pocket, get in touch with Mr. Jacobs right away.

2. The instructor will read the following mini-lecture to the class. At the end of the reading, he will give a brief quiz to check your listening efficiency.

How Sounds are Produced and Heard

For sound to be produced, there must be an energy source and a vibrating body. When we pluck a guitar string our fingers serve as the energy source and the guitar string serves as the vibrating body. As the plucked guitar string vibrates back and forth at a certain number of double-vibrations (cycles) per second, it sets air particles into motion in a series of compressions and rarefactions that are called sound waves. These sound waves are a certain amplitude and frequency, depending on the length, diameter, and tenseness of the guitar string. They are "broadcast" through the air at the relatively slow speed of 1100 feet per second.

If there is an ear within hearing distance, which is one or two hundred feet for this comparatively guiet sound, the sound waves will enter the outer ear canal and cause the eardrum to vibrate at the same frequency and amplitude as the guitar string. For example, if the guitar string is vibrating at a frequency of 256 cycles per second, the eardrum will vibrate at 256 cycles per second.

Attached to the inner side of the eardrum is a tiny bone called the *hammer*, which is attached to a second bone called the *anvil*, which, in turn, is attached to a third bone called the *stirrup*. The stirrup is attached to a membranous tissue, called the *oval window*, which separates the middle ear from the inner ear—the *cochlea*. When the eardrum is vibrated by the received sound waves, the vibration is transmitted to the three tiny bones in the middle ear, which in turn transmit the vibration of the eardrum to the oval window. The vibrating oval window transmits the vibrations to a fluid contained in the inner ear. The fluid transmits the vibrations, by way of hairlike tips on certain cells to the eighth cranial nerve, which transmits the vibrations as an impulse to the brain. In the brain, the nerve impulse is perceived as a sound that has the pitch and the quality characteristics of a guitar note.

Let us review the process once more. The guitar string is plucked by our finger (energy source). The guitar string vibrates back and forth at a certain frequency, creating sound waves that are transmitted through the air, striking an eardrum. The eardrum vibrates, transmitting the sound waves, by way of tiny bones in the middle ear, to the oval window, a membrane dividing the middle ear from the inner ear. When the oval window vibrates, the fluid in the inner ear is set into motion, causing nerve impulses to be carried by the eighth cranial nerve to the brain, where the impulses are interpreted as a particular sound—that of a guitar's "A" string.

Sample Questions:

a. What are the two things needed for sound production?

b. What is a cycle in reference to a guitar string?

c. What is a sound wave?

d. What is the speed of sound?

e. What happens when the sound wave reaches the ear?

f. What is the function of the tiny bones in the middle ear?

g. How are sound waves transmitted to the inner ear?

h. How does the sound get from the oval window to the brain?

3. Three pairs of students are selected by the instructor to demonstrate empathic listening. Each pair is seated, one at a time, in front of the class. One student of each pair acts as the interviewer, the other as the interviewee. The interviewer directs a provocative question to the interviewee and then demonstrates his ability to apply empathic listening principles in handling the interview. (Each interview should last about five minutes.) After each interview the class will discuss the nature of the empathic listening utilized.

Sample Questions:

a. What is your attitude toward capital punishment?

b. What is your attitude toward abortion?

c. What is your attitude toward the Soviet Union?

Notes

1. Stewart, John, ed., *Bridges, Not Walls* (Reading, Mass.: Addison-Wesley, 1973), p. 14.

Suggested Readings

Adler, Ron and Neil Towne, *Looking Out/Looking In: Interpersonal Communication,* (San Francisco: Rinehart Press, 1975).

This is a fascinating book with many eye-catching supplementary materials—quotations, illustrations, games, tests, and projects. See Chapter 5, "Listening versus Really Hearing."

Capp, Glen R. and G. Richard Capp, Jr., *Basic Oral Communication* 2nd ed., (Englewood Cliffs, N.J.: Prentice-Hall, 1976).

See Chapter 3, "Efficient Listening and Good Communication." This chapter is especially concerned with listening in public speaking situations.

Monroe, Alan H. and Douglas Ehninger, *Principles of Speech Communication* 7th Brief Edition, (Glenview, Ill.: Scott, Foresman & Co., 1975).

See Chapter 2, "Listening: Speaker-Audience Interaction." This chapter makes suggestions to an audience on listening for maximum results.

Webb, Ralph Jr., *Interpersonal Communication: Principles and Practices,* (Englewood Cliffs, N.J.: Prentice-Hall, 1975).

See Chapter 5, "Listening and Attention." It stresses the concept of attention and identifies the factors that affect listening. Ways of improving listening habits are suggested.

Chapter 7

Interpersonal Communication

Performance Objectives

After studying chapter 7, you should be able to:

1. Define "interpersonal communication."
2. Explain the three major goals of interpersonal communication.
3. List the seven ways of achieving effective interpersonal communication.
4. Explain and give examples of self-disclosure.
5. Explain and give examples of empathic listening.
6. Describe several ways of reducing defensive behavior in others.
7. Explain the preliminary preparations for the interviewer and the interviewee.
8. List and discuss some suggestions for the actual interview from the point of view of both the interviewer and the interviewee.

Photograph by Jerald W. Rogers.

Interpersonal communication, usually defined as communication between people, is not something new. Humans have been communicating since the dawn of civilization. But something new has been added. Today, interpersonal communication is more than people communicating: it is quality communication. Let's explore the *new* interpersonal communication.

DEFINITIONS

The *Random House Dictionary of the English Language* defines "interpersonal" as: (1) existing or occurring between persons, and (2) of or pertaining to the relationship between persons. The dictionary also defines "interpersonal theory (psychology)" as "the theory that personality development and behavior disorders are related to and determined by relationships between persons."

Some speech communication texts define "interpersonal communication" in a literal or situational sense as "communication between two persons or communication among the members of a small group." Other writers in the field , however, prefer to consider interpersonal communication as a *quality* of communication that stresses interpersonal relations. In this book, we will accept the latter interpretation.

Interpersonal communication, then, is that communication between persons, especially in a one-to-one or small group situation, that:

1. establishes friendly and satisfactory relations between the persons involved;
2. leads to individual growth and maturity; and
3. leads to a better understanding of others.

All communication is purposive; that is, we communicate to seek and to give information, to strengthen and to change belief, and so on. Interpersonal communication, however, has the additional purpose of improving relations in all communication situations, whatever the specific purpose—seeking information, for example—may be.

THE GOALS OF INTERPERSONAL COMMUNICATION

To bring about friendly relations with others. Harmonious, friendly interaction with our fellow humans is obviously more desirable than a hostile, suspicious, and fearsome relationship. Effective interpersonal communication is the major avenue to harmony and goodwill.

To improve as an individual. Our mental and emotional development depends to a great extent upon our relations with others. Effective interpersonal communication will add to our knowledge and maturity, develop our sense of personal esteem, and furnish us with personal enjoyment.

To better understand others. How often do we hear the phrase "communication breakdown?" Too often! People quarrel because of misunderstandings; good friends become distant because of misinterpretations. An important goal of interpersonal communication is to *understand the other person.*

WAYS OF ACHIEVING EFFECTIVE INTERPERSONAL COMMUNICATION

Become personally involved in the communication situation

Becoming involved in the situation means that you care about the other participants; that you are ready to commit yourself wholeheartedly to the communication situation. To become involved, make appropriate self-disclosures. If you reveal something about your personal attitudes and feelings, it encourages others to reveal their attitudes and feelings, thus establishing a bond of shared personal revelations. Note, however, the word "appropriate." Self-disclosure does not mean that you divulge your intimate life, but only those items that are appropriate. You must be the judge of what is appropriate.

Be an empathic listener. Empathic listening (sometimes called active, or nonevaluative listening) helps us to better understand other communicators in an emotional, as well as intellectual, context. For example, when fellow communicators make statements that might be considered argumentative, you should encourage them, by neutral comments and uncritical questioning, to explain or expand their statements so that you can better understand their points of view in the context of their intent, past experiences, values, and so on. When you have drawn out the communicators and feel that you really understand their points of view, then you should try to paraphrase their ideas or concepts *to their satisfaction.* When that is accomplished you are justified in proceeding with the discussion.

Think of communication as meaning-centered rather than message-centered

Realize that meaning does not reside in words (the message) but in the minds of the communicators—speaker and listener—or, as one writer suggests, meaning lies between the communicators. Public speakers may prepare an excellent message, but if they fail to adequately analyze the audience, the speech may be a failure. In other words, the speaker's meaning must correspond to the meaning in the minds of the audience.

There is an anecdote about an Englishman who notes that a dog, is called *chien* in French, in Spanish, *perro*, in German, *Hund*. "But everyone knows," he muses, "that man's best friend is really called a *dog*." This illustrates that words are not things but only agreed-upon symbols that indicate a particular referent. If two or more would-be communicators do *not* agree on the usage of a particular symbol or word, communication will falter.

Become aware of the importance of nonverbal communication

Look at the person with whom you are communicating. Maintain eye contact. Watch for facial expressions, bodily movements, and non-verbal oral utterances that may give you clues to the other person's reaction to you and/or your message. These nonverbal responses are feedback that will probably be a more exact indicator of your fellow communicators' reactions than any verbal responses they may make.

As a listener, realize that you are responding to the speakers and their messages in a nonverbal manner. Try to accept the speakers as human beings and fellow communicators by both your verbal and non-verbal reactions.

Attempt to establish interpersonal trust

Consider your fellow communicators as honest, well-intentioned, cooperative persons unless their actions or previous actions have demonstrated otherwise. Even then, give them a second chance. Use self-disclosure. Trust begets trust.

Try to reduce defensive behavior in others

Describe rather than evaluate. Instead of saying that Senator X is a bum, reveal the senator's voting record.

Be problem oriented rather than control oriented. That is, be more concerned with solving the problem at hand than with running the show.

Be spontaneous rather than manipulative. Do not scheme for gratification of your personal whims.

Emphasize the equality of those involved in the communication situation rather than any status differences.

Avoid evaluations, both verbal and nonverbal.

Avoid dogmatic behavior.

Avoid appearing indifferent.

Develop self-understanding and improve your self-concept

Be aware of the reactions of others to you and your communication habits. Are the reactions positive or negative? If they are negative, can you create a more positive image? Try!

Ask a close associate to evaluate your personality characteristics. Do such evaluations agree with your own? Analyze the discrepancies, if any. What can you do to overcome negative personality characteristics?

Be introspective some of the time. "Know thyself" is still an excellent adage.

Try to better understand others

Realize that every person is an individual regardless of group affiliations.

Remember the humanity of others—that they, too, are persons with feelings, needs, and wants.

Know that "no man is an island, entire unto itself."

> The key to effective interpersonal relations is self-awareness, understanding others, and cooperation.

THE INTERVIEW

An interview is a meeting, often prearranged, in which there is an oral exchange of questions and answers for a predetermined purpose. An interview is usually between two people.* The person who guides the meeting and poses the questions is called the *interviewer,* and the person who answers the questions is called the *interviewee.* Interviews are either public or private.

Purposes of interviews

Following are some general purposes of interviews:

1. To gain information; for example, the reporter interviews politicians to get their views on the issues; the student interviews a professor to get advice on writing a term paper.
2. To give information; for example, the counselor advises students on curricular requirements; the instructor interviews students on their progress in the course.
3. To persuade. This category might involve the job interview, the sales pitch, or other business or professional encounters in which the basic purpose is to modify behavior or to determine future action.

Preparations of the interviewer

1. You should know exactly what your purpose is in conducting the interview. What do you hope to accomplish? What do you want to know?
2. Try to establish good relations with the interviewee before the interview takes place. This might be done by letter, over the phone, in a preliminary meeting, or just before the interview itself, if it is to be a public interview.
3. Plan the interview. If you are a beginner you would be wise to prepare a written outline. Also, write down some questions to ask during the interview.
4. Read up on the subject of the interview or the area of competency of

* An interview may sometimes involve several people, as on television's *Face the Nation* and *Meet the Press.*

the interviewee. In other words, do your homework! Obviously, if you plan to interview the author of a new book, you should read the book in advance.

5. If appropriate, remind the interviewee in advance of the time, date, and place of the interview.

Preparations of the interviewee

1. Find out in advance the purpose of the interview and the occasion, setting, and people involved. Who, What, Where, When, and Why?
2. Decide if there are any special points you want to make during the interview. If so, jot them down on note cards. If you wish to supplement your answers with supporting evidence, list such material with documented sources.
3. Find out all you can about your interviewer. Who is he? What is his

The job interview. (Courtesy of New York University.)

background? What is his philosophy or point of view? What is he trying to do?

4. Confirm the time, date and place.

Suggestions for the actual interview

For the interviewer:

1. Establish good relations with the interviewee. If the interview is in your domain—your office, for example—make the interviewee feel at home. See that he is comfortably seated facing your desk so that writing facilities, ash trays, and so on are available. Smile, relax, be friendly!

2. Begin the interview with some social remarks unconnected with the purpose of the interview.

3. Begin the interview proper by stating the purpose of the interview. This may be followed by a specific question.

4. When questioning:
   a. Use open questions that require a detailed answer.
   b. Avoid closed questions that require a specific answer or a yes–no response.
   c. Ask one question at a time. Give the interviewee plenty of time to answer fully. Encourage him to expand on his answers.
   d. Avoid loaded or leading questions such as, "Don't you think we ought to lower taxes?"

5. Avoid arguing. This is not a debate.

6. When you have covered all your planned questions, bring the interview to an end. Thank the interviewee for his cooperation.

For the interviewee:

1. Dress appropriately, especially if the interview is to be held at a place other than yours.

2. Greet the interviewer warmly. If the interview is taking place in your domain, make the interviewer feel at home.

3. During the interview, be cooperative. Specifically:
   a. Answer the questions frankly and honestly.
   b. Do not be evasive, shy or negative.

   c. On the other hand, do not be over-talkative. Do not ramble.

   d. Do not be argumentative.

4. Let the interviewer set the pace and establish the mood. After all, it's his show.

General suggestions for interviewer and interviewee

1. Use simple, clear words and simple sentence structure.
2. Use an appropriate loudness level and a moderate speech rate.
3. Be animated, concerned. Get involved!
4. Use a pleasant vocal quality. Don't whine. Don't be dull. Avoid sarcasm.
5. As a listener, pay attention. Be concerned.
6. Be aware of nonverbal communication. Actions speak louder than words.
7. Be friendly, courteous, and outgoing.

> A carefully planned interview
> is the best interview.

COMMUNICATION BREAKDOWN

There are many causes for communication breakdown, among them inadequate speaking habits, poor listening habits, interference, and inappropriate language. But we would like to consider the problems encountered when two people are conversing on two different personality levels, at cross-purposes. This approach to communication breakdown is called transactional analysis, or TA for short.

Transactional analysis

TA theory was developed by the late Eric Berne (*Games People Play*). It was then popularized by Thomas A. Harris, (*I'm OK; You're OK*). Another book on TA that is quite popular in the classroom is *Born To Win*, by Muriel James and Dorothy Yongeward.

According to TA theory, everyone's personality is composed of three parts, called ego states. An ego state is a system of feelings and experiences related to the pattern of behavior that individuals develop as they grow up. The three states are **parent, adult,** and **child** (PAC). When people feel and act as their parents did, they are said to be in the parent ego state. When they think and act rationally, gathering facts, estimating probabilities, and evaluating results, they are said to be in the adult ego state. When they feel and act as they did when children, they are said to be in the child ego state. Note the similarity of these three states to the concepts developed by Freud: superego, norms imposed by society; ego, rational behavior; and id, unreasoned, instinctual behavior.

Although there are various levels of the **parent** and **child,** for the time being we will consider too much of either as being undesirable and strive for more of the **adult** in our personalities. This is not to say that we wish to eliminate our **parent** and **child** personalities, but rather to control them and use them when appropriate.

Generally, our PAC personalities are revealed by verbal expressions, but they may be revealed by our nonverbal communications as well. Following are some typical nonverbal and verbal patterns of each of the three types.

Parent

NONVERBAL: Furrowed brow, pursed lips, pointing finger, hands on hips, patting on head, sighing, tongue clucking.

VERBAL: "I'm going to put a stop to this once and for all!" "Now, always remember never to do this again." "How many times have I told you. . . ?" "If I were you. . ." Many evaluative words, whether critical or supportive, identify the parent's speech: naughty, lazy, shocking, ridiculous, disgusting, asinine, nonsense, absurd, poor thing, poor dear, sonny, honey, no! no!

Child

NONVERBAL: Tears, quivering lip, pouting, temper tantrums, high-pitched whining voice, rolling eyes, shrugging shoulders, downcast eyes, teasing, laughing, delight, thumbing nose, raising hand for permission, squirming, and giggling.

VERBAL: "I wish," "I want," "I dunno," "I gonna," "I don't care," "big," "bigger," "biggest.""When I grow up," "Look Dad, no hands."

Adult

NONVERBAL: Facial expressiveness achieved by continual movement, rapid eyeblinking. Does not look blank, dull, or insipid.

VERBAL: "Why," "what," "where," "when," "who," "how," "how much," "in what way," "comparative," "true," "false," "probably," "possible," "unknown," "objective."

The four life positions

1. *I'm not OK; you're OK* is the universal position of early childhood.
2. *I'm not OK; you're not OK* is the position of someone who feels abandoned, gives up, who won't do anymore stroking.
3. *I'm OK; you're not OK* is the criminal's position; it is a characteristic of battered children.
4. *I'm OK; you're OK* is the adult position and is based on thought, reason, faith.

TA diagrams

Diagrams are used in TA theory to demonstrate the difference between a complementary transaction and a crossed transaction in a one-to-one communication. Figure 7–1 illustrates several instances of complementary transactions; Figure 7–2 shows crossed transactions.

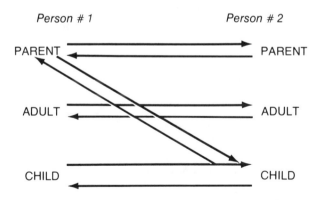

FIGURE 7–1.
Complementary transactions.

Complementary transactions

1. P to P   These trains are always late.
   P to P   Never knew it to fail.
2. A to A   What time is it?
   A to A   Four-thirty.
3. C to C   I wish I were a millionaire.
   C to C   Me, too!
4. P to C   Be sure to write!
   C to P   I will, Mom.

Crossed transactions

1. A to A   Have you seen my tie, dear?
   P to C   It's where you left it.

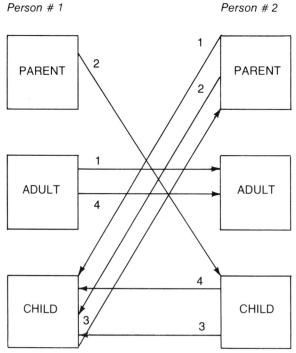

FIGURE 7–2.
Crossed transactions.

2. p to c   You ought to study more.
    p to c   Mind your own business.
3. c to p   Is it alright if I watch television?
    · c to c   Questions, questions, questions!
4. a to a   I like your suit.
    c to c   I'll bet you tell that to all the guys.

How would you diagram the following?

1. I think I would enjoy being a teacher.
    You can't even take care of your own kids.

2. What was the assignment for Friday?
    What will you give me if I tell you?

3. Let's cut class today.
    Don't be stupid, Charlie.

4. Could I borrow a cigaret?
    Smoking is bad for your health.

5. Don't stay out too late, dear!
    Now, mother, I am twenty-one, you know!

6. What time is it?
    Daytime, that's what!

> Avoid crossed transactions!
> (Who's saying that?)

Projects

1. Several pairs of students demonstrate appropriate self-disclosure and nonverbal communication to the class.

2. Pairs demonstrate information-seeking interviews and obtain information about the interviewee's early life, vocational plans, and hobbies. All class members should participate in this project, both as interviewer and interviewee.

3. Pairs demonstrate empathic listening to the class as follows: One member of each pair asks a question about a controversial subject such as, "What is your attitude toward prostitution?" When the second member of the pair answers, the questioner demonstrates his ability to empathize by encouraging the other to elaborate so that the questioner can really understand the partner's thoughts and feelings. Then the questioner will paraphrase the partner's point of view to the partner's satisfaction. All members of the class should participate.

4. Working in pairs, students demonstrate a hypothetical job interview. Each pair will determine in advance the details of the situation, for example, the hiring firm, the line of work, and the description of the job to be filled.

5. Each student prepares ten examples of dialogue demonstrating crossed transactions in TA. The class will hear the transactions and determine the PAC personalities involved in each transaction.

Suggested Readings

Adler, Ron and Neil Towne, *Looking Out/Looking In: Interpersonal Communication,* (Corte Madera, Calif: Rinehart Press, 1975).

This is a fascinating book with all kinds of stimulating interpersonal devices. We suggest you read the entire book.

Brooks, William D., *Speech Communication,* 2nd ed., (Dubuque: William C. Brown Co., 1974).

Speech Communication is a comprehensive text that has sections on intrapersonal, interpersonal, public, and cross-cultural communication. It is quite suitable for the reader who wishes to "touch all bases" in speech communication.

DeVito, Joseph H., *The Interpersonal Communication Book*, (New York: Harper & Row, 1976).

This book is divided into forty-two units on interpersonal communication. It is well organized and quite readable.

Keltner, John W., *Interpersonal Speech Communication, Elements and Structures*, (Belmont, Calif: Wadsworth Pub., Co., 1970).

This text covers the basic concepts of interpersonal communication plus interviewing, small group discussion, public speaking, oral reading and theatre.

Larson, Charles D., *Communication: Everyday Encounters*, (Belmont, Calif.: Wadsworth Pub. Co., 1976).

Communication covers interpersonal communication and has chapters on group encounters, public encounters, mass media, and cultural communication. It stresses contemporary forms of communication—television, programming, mass media advertising, popular music, and art.

McCroskey, James C., Carl E. Larson and Mark L. Knapp, *An Introduction to Interpersonal Communication*, (Englewood Cliffs, N.J.: Prentice-Hall, 1971).

One of the earliest texts on interpersonal communication, this book contains materials on interpersonal communication theory plus chapters on interpersonal communication in marriage, on the job, and in mass communication. The book has a wealth of references following each chapter.

Stewart, John, ed., *Bridges, Not Walls*, (Reading, Mass.: Addison-Wesley Pub., Co., 1973).

A forerunner of the interpersonal movement, *Bridges, Not Walls* is an excellent introduction to interpersonal communication. The balance of the text consists of articles by numerous writers on such subjects as communication as transaction, empathic listening, self-disclosure, self-perception, perceiving others, and nonverbal language. Martin Buber, Carl Rogers, Eric Fromm, and Charles M. Kelly are just a few of the authors included in this interesting text.

Webb, Ralph Jr., *Interpersonal Speech Communication: Principles and Practices*, (Englewood Cliffs, N.J.: Prentice-Hall, 1975).

This is an excellent, well-written textbook on speech communication from an interpersonal approach. It includes basic speech communication information plus chapters on one-to-one speaking, small-group discussion, public speaking and the mass media. It is recommended as supplementary reading.

Part Two
Group
Discussion

Chapter 8

Logic and Research

Performance Objectives

After studying chapter 8, you should be able to:

1. List and explain the two major types of contentions and their subdivisions. Cite examples of each.
2. Explain and illustrate the three types of evidence.
3. Explain and illustrate the two major forms of reasoning.
4. Explain arguments of example, analogy, sign, and classification as they relate to inductive and deductive reasoning.
5. Explain the table of argument patterns used for most contentions.
6. Distinguish between logical arguments and arguments from authority.
7. Explain and give examples of fallacies of evidence.
8. Explain and give examples of fallacies of inductive reasoning.
9. Explain and give examples of fallacies of deductive reasoning.
10. Explain special fallacies.
11. List and explain the special fallacies listed by the Institute of Propaganda Institute, Inc.
12. List and explain three general sources of speech materials.
13. List and discuss six or more indexes of printed materials.
14. List and discuss six or more reference sources on various subjects.
15. Explain the various tests of evidence: source, general, and statistics.

Photograph by Jerald W. Rogers.

Any communication intended to persuade, whether it is oral or written, makes certain statements or claims that the listener or reader is expected to agree with or accept as true. Often, such statements are controversial and you will have to judge them. Before you can agree, disagree, or withhold judgment on any claim, you should analyze it to determine what type of claim, or *contention*, it is and to what extent it is supported by evidence and logical reasoning. Statements in persuasive discourse may be classified as shown in Table 8–1.

TABLE 8–1. Statements in Persuasive Discourse.

Type of Contention	Examples
Statement of alleged fact	
Designative	Washington was our first president.
Definitive	A triangle is a three-sided figure.
Personal	I have a headache.
Statement of opinion	
Past or present probability	
Designative	There is life on other planets.
Effect to cause	The flood was caused by the rains.
Prediction	
Designative	Our candidate will win in November.
Cause to effect	The rains will cause a flood.
Value statement	Mary is beautiful.
Policy statement	Marijuana should be legalized.

A *designative fact statement* claims that something* does or did exist. It must be possible to confirm the statement (usually by observation) or it must have been confirmed.

A *definitive fact statement* names, describes, or classifies something. It must be possible to confirm the statement or it must have been confirmed.

A *personal fact statement* reveals some inner condition, feeling, or thought of the person making the statement. Note that this type of statement cannot be confirmed and, therefore, cannot be analyzed or judged.

A *past or present designative probability statement* claims that something exists or did exist. However, the claim cannot be confirmed, so the statement, therefore, is classified as an opinion statement.

An *effect to cause statement* is a probability statement. It claims that a particular effect was the result of a particular cause. Some cause and effect relationships are almost certain, but since cause and effect cannot be observed, we must classify these statements as opinions.

A *predictive designative statement* says that some event will probably take place in the future. A predictive statement may be just a guess or it may be a logical conclusion, based on evidence.

A *value statement* is one that describes something as good or bad, right or wrong, desirable or undesirable. Value statements often have ethical or moral implications and are often dependent upon individual standards.

A *policy statement* is one that supports a future action or policy. Such words as "should" or "ought" are often included or implied in a policy statement and are a clue to their identification. Debate topics are usually framed as policy resolutions: for example, Be it resolved, that the Equal Rights Amendment (ERA) should be ratified by the states.

USE OF THE CLASSIFICATION OF STATEMENTS

In our classification, only designative and definitive alleged fact statements can be labeled as either true or false. This means that if someone makes an alleged fact statement and we can confirm it by observation or it has been confirmed by others, we can accept the alleged statement as true with a reasonable degree of certainty. (We must keep in mind, however, the general semantic concept that truth is

*Any form of life (for example, a human being, creature, or plant), a relationship, an object, an action, a condition, and so on.

relative since it is abstracted by humans.) The other seven types of contentions, however, are only possible or probable and must be "proven" or "judged" by applying the toughest tests of logic available.

SUPPORTING CONTENTIONS WITH EVIDENCE AND REASONING

In any persuasive message, some or all of the claims may be unacceptable to the reader or listener unless they are adequately supported by evidence and logical reasoning. *Evidence* consists of facts, statements of fact, and opinions used to reach a logical conclusion. *Reasoning* is the logical-mental process of using evidence to reach a conclusion. There are two general kinds of reasoning, *inductive and deductive*.

Inductive reasoning is reasoning from the particular to the general. This is the type of reasoning that pollsters use in predicting future events. They "sample" the population and make a generalization based on the sample. In effect, they examine a small percentage of cases or instances and then predict that a much larger segment of the class (in this case the population) will have the same characteristics as the sample.

Deductive reasoning is reasoning from a general rule or accepted principle to a specific conclusion. This type of reasoning is formally stated as a syllogism, which takes the form

All men are mortal

Socrates is a man

Therefore, Socrates is mortal

Note, however, that the general truth that all men are mortal has been proved to us inductively; that is, by observing that many people have died.

Specific methods of reasoning to establish proof

1. Logical arguments.
   a. From example.   (Inductive)
   b. From analogy.   (Inductive)
   c. From sign.   (Deductive)
   d. From classification.   (Deductive)
2. Argument from authority: use of expert opinion.

An *example* is a sampling of a substance or class of things that may or may not be typical of the substance or class. An apple is an example of apples. An individual voter is an example of voters in general. If enough examples are studied, we may be able to generalize about the total class they represent. Statistics, which is data expressed numerically, is a special form of example. Reasoning from example is inductive because it uses particular cases, or samples, to reach a general conclusion.

An *analogy* is a comparison of an object or event with a similar object or event. If we observe that the two are similar in some respects, we reason that they will be alike in other, unobserved respects. This is a type of inductive reasoning because we observe a few like characteristics of two items and generalize regarding the unobserved characteristics.

A *sign* is an indication of something related to that which we observe. A knock on the door (sign) may indicate that someone is at the door. Smoke (sign) may indicate a fire. This is deductive reasoning since we have already established that a particular sign is associated with something related to that sign.

Support contentions with evidence. (Courtesy of Bryn Mawr College.)

An *argument from classification* assumes that what is generally true of a group of similar individuals will also be true of each individual in that group. "He is a Vermonter and, therefore, probably a Republican," since most residents of that state are Republican. This is also deductive reasoning since we proceed from the general to the specific.

Argument from authority is the use of opinion as evidence for a conclusion. This type of reasoning is used with logical reasoning or when facts are unavailable. The education and experience of the authority used must be acceptable to the reader or listener. Table 8–2 summarizes which patterns may be used for which contentions.

TABLE 8–2. Argument Patterns Used for the Several Contentions.

Contentions	Example	Analogy	Sign	Classifi- cation	Authority
Designative fact	x	x	x	x	x
Definitive fact	x	x		x	x
Past-present probability	x	x	x	x	x
Causal relation	x	x	x	x	x
Value statement	x	x			x
Policy statement		x			x

Justification for reasoning from accepted data to a conclusion

Arriving at any conclusion not based on observation alone requires taking a "logical leap" into the unknown. Thus, we use available facts, past experiences, or analogy to form a judgment. Evaluations and predictions based on such evidence are examples of reasoning, of taking a "logical leap" into the unknown. But we cannot use a particular pattern of argument unless we have some justification for using that particular pattern. (See Table 8-3, p. 135.) To see how a pattern of argument is developed in relation to a contention, see Figure 8-1, p. 136.

TABLE 8–3. Justification for Choosing an Argument Pattern.

Argument Pattern	Justification
Example	If one or more samples of a class of things shows certain characteristics, it is likely that others of that class will have the same or similar characteristics.
Analogy	Things that are similar in certain observed respects are likely to be similar in other, unobserved respects.
Sign	If something is observed that might be considered a part or an indication of something else, it is probable that what is indicated does or did exist.
Classification	If most of a class of things show certain characteristics, a member of the class that we do not know will tend to be the same as those we do know.
Argument from authority	When facts are unavailable, it is often necessary to seek the opinion of an authority to "prove" a contention. This is justified on the grounds that the expert, by education and experience, will have special insights into the problem.

FALLACIES

Although a strict *logical* definition of fallacy would limit the use of the term to errors in reasoning, we will generalize the definition in this book to include faulty evidence as a type of fallacy.

Fallacies of evidence

1. Untrue claims stated as facts are fallacies of evidence. We are all familiar with this fallacy. We must constantly be on our guard against deceit in persuasion. We must learn to check doubtful claims by consulting other sources and our own common sense.

2. Unjustified opinions are judgments made without examining the facts (prejudice); or lay opinion masquerading as expert opinion.

Fallacies of reasoning

1. Faulty induction.
    a. When too few examples are the basis for a generalization, the induction is faulty. "The train was late this morning, therefore the railroad must be mismanaged." "Looks like a Republican victory—at least Charlie and Jane are voting Republican."
    b. Generalizing from unrepresentative examples is another fallacy of

There is a need for a federal tax-sharing program for the states, because: (Value statement)

1. Many states are operating at a loss.	(Fact statement)
a. Florida has a deficit.*	(Example)
b. New York has a deficit.	(Example)
c. Georgia has a deficit.	(Example)
d. Thirty-one other states report financial difficulties.	(Statistics)
2. Many cities are unable to provide adequate services to their citizens because of a lack of revenue.	(Value and cause–effect statement)
a. Mayor Lindsay reports inadequate operating revenue.**	(Example)
b. Mayor Stokes reports same for Cleveland.†	(Example)
c. Other similar cities would have similar problems.	(Analogy)

And, therefore, there is a need for a federal tax-sharing program for the States.

*Items a-d from the *New York Times, December 5, 1969.* (Fact statement used to support items a-d.)

**New York Times,* January 4, 1970.
†*Plain Dealer,* January 4, 1970, Ohio.

FIGURE 8–1.
Sample contention with argumentative proof.

induction. "I talked to ten people and they all agreed that the train service was poor." (The people interviewed did not use the railroad.)

    c. Induction may also be improperly used with weak analogies. Using comparisons to prove a point when the differences in the two items are greater that the similarities is the most common misuse of analogy. "How can you expect a criminal to reform? A leopard can't change its spots."

2. Faulty deduction takes many forms, each of which has a technical name. Our concern, however, is not to name the fallacy but to be aware that a particular conclusion does not follow from the premises. For example, suppose that a friend remarks, "John must be successful; after all, he's a college graduate." Aside from the vagueness of the word "successful," it is obvious that not all college graduates achieve what they want; hence, we recognize the statement as a fallacy of deduction.

Special fallacies

1. The fallacy of irrelevency means not answering the question at issue. Any line of argument that seeks to avoid the question or the issues is a fallacy of irrelevency. Some fallacies of this type have been listed by the Institute of Propaganda Analysis, Inc.

    a. *Name calling*: "If my opponents believe that, they must be communists."

    b. *Glittering generality*: "Every American supports the president's foreign policy."

    c. *Transfer*: A speaker has the American flag draped over the lectern. The assumption is made that the speaker must be a true patriot because he displays the flag.

    d. *Plain folk*: When politicians wear coonskin hats, kiss babies, and plant seeds, they are being "plain folk." It doesn't make them better leaders.

    e. *Card stacking*: Presenting only one side of an issue.

    f. *Band wagon*: "Everybody is voting for Brown. Don't be on the losing side; vote for Brown." This does not prove that Brown is the better candidate.

2. Fallacies of unwaranted assumption.

    a. *Begging the question* means assuming true what must be proved, for example: "Since the food-stamp program encourages laziness, it should be abolished."

b. *Arguing in a circle*: "Criminals get their just dessert. People that have trouble must be criminals."

c. *Dividing the question (black or white fallacy)*: "Either we conserve gasoline or we will be walking to work in ten years." There may be other forms of energy developed within ten years.

Tests of evidence

1. Tests of the source of the evidence.
    a. Is the source of the evidence given?
    b. Is the source qualified to observe and report the facts? Is the source qualified to be an authority in matters of opinion?
    c. Was the observer physically able to clearly witness the claimed fact?
    d. Was the claim supported by other observers?
    e. Is the source up to date and aware of recent studies?
2. General tests of evidence.
    a. Does the claim seem probable? Is it supported by your past experience and common sense?
    b. Is the claimed fact still observable? Can you check it personally?
    c. Is the evidence relevant to the conclusions drawn?
    d. Is there enough evidence to justify the conclusion?
3. Tests of statistics.
    a. What is meant by the unit employed? "He has a 30 db hearing loss." Do you know the meaning of *db?*
    b. Are the units compared actually comparable? "Five students in the first class failed the exam but only 10 percent of the students in the second class failed." Can a number be compared to a percentage here?
    c. Is the time period of the statistics relevant? "Five percent of the work force is unemployed." When was the survey made?
    d. Do the statistics cover a sufficient number of cases? As the saying goes, "One swallow does not a summer make."
    e. Were the statistics gathered and prepared objectively? Who conducted the survey? Did the investigators have anything to gain from the outcome of the survey?

> Beware of propaganda and know how to deal with it.

RESEARCH TECHNIQUES

Who, what, how, when, where, and why are the six key questions of the alert reporter. The answers to these questions result in information, in knowledge. In every situation, every phase of life, we need and use information. In most communication situations, we either seek information or give it. But where do we look for information? What are the sources of information?

Three general sources of information

Our own personal knowledge and experiences are an important source of information. As we grow up, we collect information in various ways. Personal experiences, oral information from others, and reading yield information. We remember much of this knowledge and use it when necessary.

Oral information from others is the information we receive by listening to others. This information may be learned in an interview, lecture, group discussion, or even in casual conversation. Also, the radio, theater, and television may be considered sources of oral information.

Written materials such as books, magazines, documents, journals, and newspapers are the major source of written information. Since our personal libraries are usually limited, we must depend largely on college and public libraries for written information.

In searching for information of all kinds, we should use all three general sources: personal experiences, oral information, and written information. We should determine what we already know about the subject. Then we should consult others, interview them and attend lectures. Finally, we should go to the library. Get acquainted with the resources of your library. It's an invaluable source of information.

> Happiness is knowing your local librarian.

LIBRARY RESOURCES

Your library contains many books, periodicals, pamphlets, and sometimes, films and recordings that can be of great help to you in your research. The trick is, how do you locate the material you are seeking? Following are some suggested sources of library materials.

Book indexes

1. The card catalogue is the obvious "first source" of library materials. The card catalogue contains card references to all the books in the library. They are listed by author, title, and subject.

2. *Books in Print,* is a two-volume reference book listing over 300,000 books by their authors and titles. It is published annually.

3. *Cumulative Book Index,* is a monthly index of all books published in the English language. It also contains a selected list of government documents.

4. *Publisher's Weekly* lists new books.

Newspaper and periodical indexes

1. The *New York Times Index,* is based on each day's last edition. It is published twice a month and is a valuable index for current affairs.

2. The *Newspaper Index* is published monthly from microfilmed editions of the *Chicago Tribune, Los Angeles Times,* the *New Orleans Times Picayune,* and *Washington Post.* The items are indexed by subject and name.

3. *Reader's Guide to Periodical Literature* indexes most of the popular, nontechnical periodicals in the English language by author and subject. It is issued semimonthly, monthly in July and August.

4. *Social Sciences and Humanities Index,* formerly called the *International Index,* is compiled quarterly. It covers articles published in such fields as speech, literature, art, and religion.

5. The *Education Index,* indexes the contents of about 170 educational journals by author and subject.

6. The *Vertical File Index,* is an index to selected pamphlets in various fields. It lists many free or inexpensive pamphlets. It is issued monthly except in August.

Reference works

1. Encyclopedias
   a. *Encyclopedia Americana,* thirty volumes.
   b. *Encyclopaedia Britannica,* twenty-four volumes.
   c. *Collier's Encyclopedia,* twenty volumes.
   d. *Encyclopedia of the Social Sciences,* fifteen volumes.
2. Biographical Dictionaries
   a. *Who's Who* (Mainly living British notables.)
   b. *Who's Who in America*
   c. *International Who's Who*
   d. *Directory of American Scholars*
   e. *Current Biographies* (International in scope.)
   f. *Dictionary of American Biography*

3. Books of Fact
    a. *World Almanac*
    b. *Statesman's Yearbook*
    c. *Information, Please, Almanac*
    d. *Statistical Abstracts of the United States.*
4. Dictionaries
    a. *Random House Dictionary of the English Language,* Unabridged, 1966 (260,000 words).
    b. *Webster's Third New International Dictionary of the English Language,* Unabridged, 1961 (almost 500,000 words).

RECORDING INFORMATION

When researching a subject, always record your research finding. Do not trust your memory! Although there is no "right way" to record information, we suggest that four-by-six inch cards be used. A card system will make it easy for you to sort out and reuse information for later group discussion, public speaking, or debate. Our method of taking notes on cards has proven helpful to students in the past.

1. Indicate the general subject area in the upper righthand corner of the card. For example, "UNEMPLOYMENT."
2. Indicate the specific topic in the upper lefthand corner of the card. For example "CAUSES OF" (unemployment).
3. Write the bibliographical information on the top line of the card. Include the author, title of book or article, publisher, date and page number. For example, Zelko, Harold, *The Business Conference,* New York: McGraw-Hill Book Co., 1969, p. 14.
4. Paraphrase or quote the desired material in the remaining space on the card. Use facts, statistics, tables, research findings, summaries, and the like. Condense, abbreviate, paraphrase, summarize. Get as much data on one subject as you can on a single card.
5. If more than one card is necessary for one source, number the additional cards 1–A, 1–B, and so on, and label them with the main topic, specific topic, and an abbreviated form of the bibliographical material. For example, Zelko, *Business Conference.*

6. When you have completed your research, sort your cards according to specific topics. In group discussion, these topics would probably be the objectives of the discussion agenda, or, in public speaking, the main items of your outline. If, for example, the major subject is unemployment, your specific topics might be (1) The nature of the unemployment, (2) The extent of unemployment, (3) Causes of unemployment, and (4) Suggested solutions. See Figure 8–2 for an example of what your research card should look like.

Management Philosophy   UNEMPLOYMENT
   (*Specific topic*)   (*General topic*)
Zelko, Harold, *The Business Conference,* NY: McGraw-Hill, 1969, p.14.
   (*Bibliography*)

"The basic communication 'dilemmas' for business are the problem of social climate and the problem of technology versus human factors. In both, choices based on judgment must be made. And these choices produce a combination of management philosophy, prevailing concepts, orall climate, and day-to-day practices which are the basis for the communication goals of any organization. The emergence of group process and conferences as the primary—perhaps inevitable—tools for the accomplishment of these goals is the reason for this book."

FIGURE 8–2.
Sample research card.

Projects

1. Working in groups of three, prepare two sentences per group for each of the nine types of contentions. Each group presents examples of one type of contention to the class. The examples are followed by general discussion and, hopefully, agreement, before the next type of contention is examined.

2. Each group presents explanations and examples of one or more of the following:
   a. The three types of evidence.
   b. The major forms of reasoning.
   c. The syllogism.
   d. Reasoning from example, analogy, sign, and classification.
   e. Reasoning from authority.

3. Each student selects a topic for a hypothetical discussion and prepares five four-by-six inch cards listing the general topic, specific topic, and bibliographical information. Five different reference indexes must be used. The card catalogue, *New York Times Index*, *Reader's Guide to Periodical Literature*, *Education Index*, and *Social Sciences and Humanities Index*, are good choices. The bibliographical information will, of course, be different for each card. Write the name of the index used on the body of the card.

4. Each student prepares two complete cards from two different reference sources such as encyclopedias. Each card must include the major topic, specific topic, bibliographical line, and the research date on the body of the card.

Suggested Readings

Cohen, Morris, R. and Ernest Nagel, *An Introduction to Logic and Scientific Method*, (New York: Harcourt, Brace & Co., 1934).

This book has a challenging approach to logic and scientific method. It is a classic in the field.

Copi, Irving M., *Introduction to Logic*, 3rd ed., (New York: The MacMillan Co., 1968).

This is a readable book on traditional logic.

Ehninger, Douglas and Wayne Brockriede, *Decision by Debate*, (New York: Dodd, Meade and Co., 1963).

Decision by Debate has an excellent summary of library research facilities and research recording suggestions.

Mills, Glen E., *Reason in Controversy*, (Boston: Allyn and Bacon, Inc., 1968).

This book is a good summary of "debate logic" based on the leading textbooks on argumentation and debate.

Tandberg, Gerily, *Research Guide in Speech*, (Morristown, N.J.: General Learning Press, 1974).

Research Guide in Speech is a detailed report on library research facilities, especially as applicable to the study of speech communication.

THREE HEADS (OR MORE)

ARE BETTER THAN ONE!

Photograph by Jerald W. Rogers.

Chapter 9

Group Discussion

Performance Objectives

After studying chapter 9, you should be able to:

1. Define group discussion and distinguish it from casual social conversation.
2. Explain the difference between private and public group discussion and between formal and informal group discussion.
3. Discuss the four purposes or functions of group discussion.
4. Explain the following concepts: conference, committee, panel, symposium, lecture–forum, open meeting.
5. List and explain the five suggestions for selecting a topic for discussion.
6. List and explain the seven rules for wording a discussion topic.
7. Explain the meaning of "task functions" and "maintenance functions."
8. Explain the concepts: group structure, group norms, cohesiveness, task commitment.
9. Explain the three factors of individual behavior in the group situation. Explain "role playing."
10. Explain the four phases of interaction in group discussion.

149

WHAT IS DISCUSSION?

People often get together to talk things over. The popular term for this type of meeting is *group discussion*. However, *discussion*, as used in this text, does not mean casual, chance conversation, but implies a planned meeting that has a definite purpose. Exchanging information, solving a common problem, satisfying a need, are purposes of discussion. Thus, a family group would get together to "discuss" vacation plans; a fraternity council would meet to discuss membership policy; a college faculty group, to discuss a curriculum change; or a group of citizens, to consider raising school taxes. In all walks of life, discussion is a very practical and democratic way of achieving certain goals.

Discussions not only have various functions but take several forms. They may be *private;* that is, of specific concern to the participating members or *public;* that is, intended for an audience that may or may not participate. Discussions may be *formal,* with prepared speeches or *informal,* with a random exchange of ideas and suggestions.

Discussion meetings are usually conducted by a *moderator* who is sometimes referred to as a *chairperson* or *leader.* Some discussion groups meet with little advance preparation; others, after considerable preparation. In the latter case, the group may determine in advance the research needs of the discussion, and the moderator may assign specific research tasks to each member of the group in preparation for the actual discussion. When research is undertaken in this manner, it is called *cooperative research.*

> Discussion is the oral exchange of ideas between three or more people, usually under the direction of a leader, for the purpose of enlightenment, solving a common problem, or satisfying a felt need.

PURPOSES OF DISCUSSION

One reason people meet for discussion is *to determine the action to be taken regarding a problem or need of the group.* This probably is the most important function of discussion. For example, let's assume that the Department of English at your college wishes to consider the desirability of sponsoring an essay contest. A meeting of the department is called and the discussion that follows might cover (1) the benefits of such a contest, (2) the details of the contest, and (3) ways of implementing the contest.

In other words, the purpose or reason for holding the discussion would be to initiate *action* toward fulfilling a need of the group.

Another reason for discussion is *to formulate policy or establish attitudes.* Often, a discussion might be held to determine policy or to decide attitudes toward a particular issue or problem. For example, such problems as crime, disease, slums, and war are good, basic topics for discussions of policy. Such discussions might be followed by direct action in the form of signing petitions, voting, and legislation.

A discussion group may also meet for the purpose of *exchanging information.* For example, a college course is often taught through discussion. Employees are sometimes instructed in the use of new equipment through this method.

In other instances, however, the exchange of information may be only one phase of a broader discussion. In problem-solving discussions there will be a phase of the discussion devoted to the *investigation, organization,* and *presentation*—or actual exchange—of factual material.

Promoting better understanding between groups with different interests is another reason for discussion. Often, discussion can bring about harmony and cooperation between "opposing" groups such as management and labor, government and industry, faculty and students, or even husbands and wives.

A valuable by-product of participation in discussion is that it trains the individual in *objective listening, effective self-expression,* and *cooperative thinking.* You will find this training useful in all other forms of oral communication.

> Discussion is *not* casual conversation but has a definite goal or purpose.

TYPES OF DISCUSSION

Often, the purpose or reasons for a discussion will determine the type or form of discussion. For example, if a student organization wants to plan its program for the following year, a small private conference might be in order. On the other hand, if the organization believes that an increase in student activity fees is needed, it might be more appropriate to hold an open, or public, meeting and invite the entire student body to attend.

Some typical formats for discussion follow:

Conference. A conference is an informal, planned discussion among three or more informed participants meeting in a face-to-face situation, usually under the direction of a moderator. The primary purpose of a conference is to find a satisfactory solution to a mutual problem or need.

Committee. A committee discussion is similar to a conference except that the group has been appointed or elected by a larger group to investigate a particular problem or to perform a specific function. Usually the committee, through its chairperson, is expected to give its findings and recommendations to the parent organization for final action. Committee meetings are usually private.

Panel. A panel is an informal discussion that involves three to nine participants under the direction of a moderator, on a question of general interest. The discussion is held before an audience and the panelists are seated so that they can be clearly seen and heard by all. A part of the meeting, usually the latter part, may be opened to the audience for questions. In this case, the discussion is called a *panel–forum.*

Symposium. The symposium is similar to the panel except that the "panelists" present formal speeches of about five to fifteen minutes each on some phase of the discussion question. If audience participation is

A panel-forum answers questions. (Courtesy of New York University.)

allowed after the formal presentations, the meeting is called a *symposium–forum*.

Lecture–forum. A lecture–forum is a talk given by an expert on a particular subject. It is followed by a discussion period involving the audience. In many cases, a moderator other than the lecturer directs the audience-participation period.

Open meeting. An open meeting is a gathering of a group for the purpose of airing grievances, clarifying policies, and so forth. The meeting is directed by a moderator and all members of the group are encouraged to participate in the discussion.

> Use that type of discussion that will best fulfill the purpose of the meeting.

THE DISCUSSION QUESTION

Selecting the topic for discussion

It was suggested that group problems or needs are especially suited to discussion methods. But how do we determine what problems or needs should be discussed? In some instances, a problem is so immediate and obvious that spontaneous discussion is unavoidable. For example, in one commuter town in New York, the railroad fare was increased 50 percent in a six-month period. Several groups immediately formed to discuss the problem and to consider other means of transportation. In other instances, a group may want to discuss methods of solving a particular social problem, such as juvenile delinquency. Or problems may arise in our business, church, or social club that can best be solved through discussion methods.

We are confronted by many problems, so it is necessary to be selective in our choice of discussion topics. A few suggestions to observe in selecting a topic:

1. Select a topic that represents an immediate, important problem to the group concerned.
2. Select a topic for which you are likely to find a satisfactory solution. For example, avoid such issues as "The probability of life after death" or "The relative merits of George Washington versus Abraham Lincoln." A discussion of such subjects can only lead to guesses or value judgments.

3. Select a topic about which information is available.

4. Select a topic that the participants are capable of discussing. For example, a lay group might find the topic "Nuclear fission" too complex for profitable discussion.

5. If the discussion is to be public, select a topic that will meet the needs and interests of the audience and will be suitable for the occasion.

> Select a topic on the basis of practical criteria.

Narrowing the topic for discussion

A *topic* may consist of only one word, for example, "Communism," "Education," "Crime," or "Disease." Obviously, these topics are too broad for profitable discussion. It is necessary to narrow the topic to a *subject* that will (1) meet the time limits of the meeting and (2) include the important aspects of the topic that the group wants to consider.

Let us try to narrow down the topic "Juvenile delinquency." First, we might narrow the geographic area of the topic to our particular community. Second, we might limit the topic to a certain group of delinquents based on age, sex, or other factors. Finally, we might limit the topic to a certain aspect of delinquency such as *preventing* juvenile delinquency, *reeducating* delinquents, and *punishing* delinquents.

> Narrow the topic to meet the time limit.

Wording the discussion subject

After selecting and narrowing the topic for discussion, we must *word* the actual discussion subject. We suggest you follow these rules:

1. Word the subject as a question. A question motivates more than a statement does because it implies that a search for answers is needed. It also promotes a search for the truth since a statement may suggest a bias. Contrast these two wordings of the topic "Juvenile delinquency."

    a. As a statement: "The punishment of high school delinquents should be more severe than it is now."

b. As a question: "How can our community best prevent juvenile delinquency among its high school students?

2. Word the question so that is allows several answers. Usually a question that calls for a yes or no is too limiting and tends to create a debate situation that defeats the spirit of discussion. Note the examples
in Table 9–1.

In some cases, however, it may be desirable to discuss a yes or no
question. When the participants are aware of other possible solutions, or when other solutions have been adequately explored, it may
be appropriate to word the question so that it may be answered
affirmatively or negatively.

3. Avoid "question-begging" words when phrasing the discussion
question. For example, in the question, "How can we bring about the
repeal of the unfair Taft–Hartley Act," the word "unfair" is question-
begging because it assumes which must be proved.

4. Avoid ambiguity in phrasing the discussion question. For example,
in the question, "How can we best control the abuse of our natural
resources?" the participants do not know who *we* refers to, the

Table 9–1. Stating the Question.

| Problem | Stating the Question | |
	Too Limited	Broader
Lack of adequate revenue	Should off-track betting be legalized?	In what way can our government raise additional revenue?
Drug addicts	Should drug addicts be treated as criminals?	What attitude should society adopt toward the drug addict?
Censorship	Should the FCC be given more power over television?	To what extent, if any, should the FCC exercise censorship over television?

significance of *control,* or the limitations of *natural resources.* This particular wording is, therefore, ambiguous.

5. Word the discussion question so that it covers one question only. For example, "How can we lower the divorce rate and bring about uniform divorce laws in the United States?" is two questions in one and must be treated as two questions.

6. When necessary, word the discussion question in such a way that it provides for dissenting opinions. For example, in the question, "To what extent should taxes be lowered in our state?" there is no provision for a dissenting opinion *against* lowering the taxes. Inserting the phrase "if at all" after the word *extent* will allow for a dissenting point of view.

7. If the discussion is to be held before an audience, it may be preferable to word the question as a "catchy" phrase that will appeal to the public. For example, one discussion on communism was advertised, "Will your child be a communist?" At the meeting, however, the question was presented as, "How can the United States best meet the challenge of communism?"

> Phrase the subject as a single question conducive to multiple solutions, free from question-begging words and ambiguity and allowing for dissent.

PREPARATION FOR AND PARTICIPATION IN THE DISCUSSION

A good discussion consists of a fruitful exchange of ideas leading to a "best" solution. Discussion should not be an exchange of ignorance. Since, in most instances, a discussion is announced in advance, there is plenty of time for all participants to prepare for the discussion by doing research on the problem beforehand. Research alone, however, will not result in effective discussion. The participants must have a working knowledge of discussion techniques and be able to speak effectively.

Each participant, including the moderator, should enter into the discussion with an open mind and an objective attitude. The participants should be courteous, friendly, and cooperative. They should keep in mind that discussion is a democratic process aimed at arriving at a best solution to a problem. Individual participants should not talk excessively or otherwise dominate the discussion session. They should listen carefully to the contributions of others and respect the opinions of all in the group. Their own contributions and disagreements should be given tactfully. The participants should keep in mind that sometimes compromise may be essential if a group is to reach consensus on a particular issue.

> Discussion is not an exchange of ignorance!

TASK FUNCTIONS AND MAINTENANCE FUNCTIONS

Participants have two basic functions in a discussion; (1) *task functions;* that is, solving the problem or fulfilling the purpose of the discussion, and (2) *maintenance functions;* that is, establishing a satisfactory atmosphere for discussion and maintaining a procedure of interaction that aids in accomplishing the task. The moderator and the participants should all be concerned with the task and maintenance functions required.

THE CHARACTERISTICS OF THE DISCUSSION GROUP

As you begin to participate in group discussion, you will probably be aware that each group has its own identity, its own characteristics.

The unique nature of each group is a product of the individual characteristics of the participants plus the structure, purpose, restraints, and so on, of the group itself. Let us examine some of the deciding factors of group characteristics.

Structure

The make-up of the group is an important determining factor in the effective functioning of the group. More specifically, we are concerned with the size of the group, the status of participants, and the discussion format.

Size. Conferences appear to function well with groups of from five to nine members. An odd number is preferred to an even number so that, in the absence of consensus, a vote can be taken. The ideal number of participants is probably five. This number encourages all to participate and yet there are five "heads" to draw upon for decision-making.

Status of participants. If the participants are on the same status level, for example, all students, there will usually be better group togetherness. More friendliness, more interaction, and fewer restraints on the participants are the results of equal status. On the other hand, if the participants are not on the same status level, every effort should be made to downplay such differences and to uphold democratic ideals during the discussion meetings.

The discussion format. The formality or informality of the discussion, the presence or absence of observers, the method of selecting a leader, and the degree of freedom will all have an effect on the characteristics of the group. Although authoritarianism may be more efficient in problem-solving, democratic procedures will prove more beneficial in the long run.

Group norms

Norms are codes of behavior that regulate interaction among the group members. Norms are not formal, as is parliamentary procedure, but are unwritten rules that are adopted by the members of a group. Members who disregard the norms are subtly encouraged, in various ways, to change their habits and abide by the "rules."

Cohesiveness

Cohesiveness is the quality of group unity, of team spirit. Cohesiveness is a most desirable trait in group discussion. It improves the morale of the participants and leads to a greater degree of task accomplishment. Cohesiveness is usually associated with the ongoing group; that is the group that meets often or perhaps on a regular basis. Also, homogeneous groups (groups of individuals of the same age level, educational background, work level, and so on) would probably develop more cohesiveness than a heterogeneous group (composed of dissimilar individuals).

Task commitment

How hard a group will try to complete a selected task is always an important characteristic of a group, but this factor is dependent upon the immediacy and importance of the problem and the rewards involved for the individual. Rewards may be peer approval, self-satisfaction, and material benefits. In a classroom situation, grades may serve as a reward, or the praise of the instructor may strengthen a student's efforts.

FORCES AFFECTING THE INDIVIDUALS IN GROUP DISCUSSION

Desire to control[1]

Although the desire to control may vary considerably from one individual to another, it is a factor that must be recognized. It can be used by the discerning moderator to implement the task goals of the group, for example, by assigning special responsibilities to the individual. If not used constructively, the desire to control can become a disruptive force in the problem-solving process.

Desire for inclusion

The need to belong, to feel a part of the group, is a strong drive in the individual. The degree of need for inclusion will, of course, be dependent upon the prestige of the group, its exclusiveness, and the expected rewards to the individual. The desire to belong to a group may vary with the manner of joining the group. Individuals assigned to a group may not want to be included. On the other hand, individuals who select their own groups will probably want to be included. The satisfaction of being included helps individuals to establish their identities.

Desire for affection

We all want to be liked, and this desire of the individual in a group is probably more constant than the desires of control and inclusion. The need for affection is generally fulfilled relatively late in the discussion situation, after the satisfaction of the desires of inclusion and control.

Role playing

Members of the group see themselves as performing one or more functions in the group. In other words, members adopt a role in the group, whether as recorder, devil's advocate, or whatever. Individuals achieve status with the other members of the group by their choice of roles and their conscientious efforts to fulfill these roles.

THE FOUR PHASES OF INTERACTION IN GROUP DISCUSSION

B. Aubrey Fisher conducted an experiment that indicates that a typical group goes through four distinct phases in the discussion process:[2]

1. During the *orientation phase* the members are concerned with getting acquainted. They are cautious and unsure in their opinions. They tend to agree with anything said, even debatable comments. This tendency to "over-agree" is attributed to the need to ease socialization.
2. During the *conflict phase* members are more assertive and positive. Attitudes are further apart, either for or against a point of view. There is

less vagueness in expressions and the expressions are more strongly held. This is the phase of controversy, argument, and dispute.

3. Conflict gradually diminishes during the *emergence phase*. Comments and proposals are interpreted more frequently and members do not defend themselves as strongly as in the conflict phase. Disagreeing attitudes are expressed more vaguely.

4. The group's preferred decisions and reinforcement in favor of them become more visible during the *reinforcement phase*. Argument is no longer important; disagreement has all but vanished. Favorable attitudes prevail and there is a spirit of general unity.

RESEARCH FINDINGS

Dickens and Heffernan suggest that the following conclusions have been well established:[3]

1. After discussion, extreme judgments tend to draw in toward a middle ground.
2. After discussion, judgments tend to improve in accuracy and/or correctness.
3. Individual judgment is greatly influenced by knowing how the majority stands.
4. Right answers tend to be held more strongly than wrong ones under the same conditions of majority agreement or opposition.
5. Groups are superior to individuals in dealing with problems permitting a greater range of responses.

Research in the field of group dynamics in discussion has been fairly recent. The results above should give you some idea of the directions being followed in current research efforts. Be aware that as individuals are different, so too are groups. Each group has its own personality.

> A knowledge of group characteristics will help you in the discussion process.

WHY SOME DISCUSSIONS FAIL

Group faults

1. Poor selection of topic.
   a. Topic depends too much on personal values: for example, "What attitude should we have toward premarital sex?"
   b. Topic is unanswerable: for example, "Is there life after death?"
   c. Little or no information available on topic: for example, "Is there human life on other planets?"
2. Topic poorly worded for discussion question.
   a. Worded as a yes or no debate question.
   b. Too broad: for example, "How can we prevent wars?"
   c. Ambiguous: for example, "How can we stop the drain on natural resources?"
3. Group doesn't know discussion techniques.
4. Group does not have knowledge needed to deal with problem.
5. Group not interested in problem.

Leader faults

1. Does not know the role of the leader.
2. Overly timid. Reluctant to lead or guide the group.
3. Lack of preparation.
4. Has not prepared an agenda.
5. Overdominant. Bossy.
6. Takes advantage of role to stress his own views.
7. Fails to encourage shy members.
8. Fails to summarize important points.
9. Has poor speech habits.
10. Is poorly groomed.

Participant faults

1. Little or no preparation.
2. Hostile attitude toward goals of group.

3. Hostile attitude toward members of group.

4. Excessive shyness or timidity.

5. Tendency to dominate, to be overtalkative.

6. Inability to be serious (the perpetual clown or comic).

7. Rigidity of opinion. Unable to adjust or compromise.

8. Hostility, loudness, threatening behavior.

9. Posture inappropriate for group norms.

10. Dress inappropriate for group norms.

11. Language inappropriate for group norms. Poor speech habits.

12. Inability to accept criticism.

13. Tendency to overreact emotionally.

14. Inclined to introduce irrelevant material.

15. Poor listener.

16. Selfish attitude.

17. Unreliable. Absent without explanation. Late. Does not complete assigned tasks.

18. Lack of knowledge of discussion techniques.

19. Uses fallacious reasoning. Illogical.

20. Laziness. Has tendency to shift responsibility to others.

Note: The materials covered in this chapter apply to all types of discussion. For a more detailed description of the problem-solving discussion, see chapter 10.

Projects

1. Select five general topics that you feel represent current problems suitable for discussion. For example: "Juvenile delinquency."
2. Narrow your five topics with appropriate wording so that each topic can be adequately discussed in a typical two-hour meeting. For example: "Juvenile delinquency among high school students in our community."
3. Phrase the five revised subjects as discussion questions, applying the suggested rules for wording the question. For example: "How can our community best prevent juvenile delinquency among its high school students?"
4. Prepare a bibliography on one or more of your discussion questions. Use the card catalogue, indexes, and reference sources available in your library.
5. Prepare four-by-six inch research cards from five different sources on one of your discussion questions.

Notes

1. William O. Schutz, *FIRO A Three-Dimensional Theory of Interpersonal Behavior*, (New York: Rinehart, 1950).
2. B. Aubrey Fisher, "Patterns of Communicative Interaction in Small Groups," *Speech Monographs*, 37 (1970), pp. 53–66.
3. Milton Dickens and Marguerite Heffernan, "Experimental Research in Group Discussion," *Quarterly Journal of Speech*, 35, (1949), pp. 23–29.

Suggested Readings

Applbaum, Ronald L. and others, *The Process of Group Communication*, (Chicago: Science Research Associates, 1974).

This book gives detailed presentation of the group-communication process. An entire chapter is devoted to each of the following: problem solving, norms and roles, cohesiveness, conflict, and leadership.

Goldberg, Alvin A. and Carl E. Larson, *Group Communication: Discussion Processes and Applications,* (Englewood Cliffs, N.J.: Prentice-Hall, 1975).

Group Communication is a good introduction to theory and research on group discussion.

Shepard, Clovis N., *Small Groups: Some Sociological Perspectives,* (San Francisco: Chandler, 1964).

This book presents various theories and research findings on the small group from the sociological point of view.

Chapter 10

The Problem-Solving Conference

Performance Objectives

After studying chapter 10, you should be able to:

1. Define "problem-solving conference."
2. List and explain the three stock objectives of the analysis phase and the four stock objectives of the solution phase.
3. List and explain the standard "debate inquiries."
4. Explain the moderator's responsibilities before the discussion. (Assume that a preliminary meeting is impossible.)
5. Explain the moderator's responsibilities during and after the meeting.
6. Explain the participants' responsibilities before and during the discussion meeting.

Photograph by Jerald W. Rogers.

DEFINITION

The problem-solving conference is a preplanned, face-to-face gathering of a small group of three to nine informed people who meet under the leadership of a moderator for the purpose of exchanging ideas in order to solve a mutual problem or satisfy a need.

Let us examine this rather involved definition in greater detail. The time and place of the discussion meeting are decided in advance. The question for discussion and the agenda for the meeting are prepared before the meeting, preferably at a preliminary meeting. The participants, individually or together, have thoroughly researched the problem before the discussion. This type of discussion differs little from other discussion types except for its emphasis on the research phase of the discussion and the "problem" nature of the discussion question.

PREPARING THE AGENDA

The agenda is an outline of goals or objectives of the discussion group. The agenda divides the discussion question into its logical parts, which can then be considered individually at one or more discussion sessions.

Since the format of many agendas is similar, the following *stock objectives,* which are suitable for many discussion questions, may serve as a guide in preparing the agenda.

STOCK OBJECTIVES

Analysis phase

1. To determine the nature of the problem.
2. To determine the extent of the problem.
3. To determine the causes of the problem.

Solution phase

4. To list possible solutions to the problem.
5. To establish suitable criteria for a best solution.

6. To select the best solution(s) to the problem.

7. To implement the selected solution(s).

The first step in any problem-solving discussion is to understand the problem. What is its history and background? Is it a new problem or a recurring problem? Is it an educational, political, social, or economic problem? Who has jurisdiction in this area?

How extensive is the problem? What are the effects of the problem? What are the statistics? How many people are involved? What is the relationship of the discussion group to the problem? What jurisdiction does the discussion group have in the problem?

In many cases, we should be more concerned with the causes of the problem than with the surface symptoms. If we can eliminate the causes of a problem, the problem itself will be eliminated.

When listing possible solutions, it is suggested that all possible solutions be listed freely, without analysis or criticism. This procedure, called "brainstorming," tends to stimulate thinking and inventiveness since a free flow of ideas tends to draw out other related ideas from the group. Also, brainstorming has the advantage of placing *all* suggested solutions before the group, allowing for a later analysis and comparison of the suggested solutions.

In this phase of the discussion, the proposed solutions should be listed on a blackboard or display pad. When all suggestions have been listed, the group may wish to combine some solutions and qualify others.

Criteria are the standards or limitations a solution must fit. For example, one criterion might be that the cost of implementing a particular solution be low. Another might have to do with the legality or constitutionality of a proposal. By establishing criteria in advance, time can be saved by rejecting those extreme proposals that do not meet the determined criteria for solutions.

Selecting the best solution(s) may be considered the "debate phase" of the discussion. The suggested solutions are analyzed, criticized, and compared until a "best" solution is selected. For example, let us assume that four solutions have been suggested to our question, "How can our community best prevent juvenile delinquency among its high school students?": (1) to increase the length of the school day by adding more extracurricular activities; (2) to hire additional school psychologists; (3) to encourage greater parental responsibility; and (4) to maintain a twenty-four-hour police guard on the school premises. These proposed solutions can now be treated as debate propositions such as, "Should we increase the length of the school day by adding more extracurricular activities?" These questions can then be analyzed and tested by applying standard debate inquiries as follows:

1. Is the proposed solution desirable?
    a. Would it lessen or eliminate the problem?
    b. Would it provide additional benefits?
    c. Would it avoid the creation of new problems?
2. Is the proposed solution practical?
    a. Can it be financed?
    b. Can it be administered?
    c. Can it be enforced?
3. Is the proposed solution the best solution? (At this point, the solution being tested is compared to other possible solutions on the basis of probable advantages and disadvantages.)

By applying these questions to each of the suggested solutions, the group should be able to select as *best* one or more of the solutions offered.

After solving the problem, how are we going to put our solution into effect? If the group has the power to act, for example, if it is a governmental body or a business organization, the recommended course of action can be put into effect at will. Sometimes the findings of a discussion group remain recommendations and can only be implemented by another group with the power to act. The recommendations should be made known to the proper authorities by letters, petition, word of mouth, and so on.

Our list of stock objectives is meant only to guide you in drawing up the specific agenda of your conference. Use the stock objectives only to the extent that they meet the needs of the problem under discussion.

> The agenda consists of the goals or objectives of the conference group.

RESPONSIBILITIES OF THE PARTICIPANTS

To assure the success of a problem-solving conference, the moderator and participants must fulfill certain responsibilities. Following is a summary of those responsibilities.

The moderator's responsibilities before the conference

The moderator has the important task of preparing for the conference in every detail. If possible, the moderator should have at least two weeks to make these preparations. If you are the moderator, use the following check list of responsibilities. (It is assumed that the members of the discussion group have already been selected and that the general topic for discussion has been chosen.

1. Do as much research on the question as time permits.
   a. Prepare a bibliography to be shared by the group.
   b. Record all research materials on four-by-six inch cards.
   c. Collect as much material to distribute to the group as is available. Reprints, pamphlets, bulletins, booklets, and reports are all good.
2. Determine which research areas require joint investigation.
3. Plan a preliminary meeting. Notify members of the time, date, place

An informal problem-solving group. (Courtesy of New York University.)

and purpose of this meeting. Include the following items on the agenda of the preliminary meeting:

a. Phrase the question for discussion.

b. Define the terms of the question.

c. Plan the agenda, or the objectives, of the discussion meeting.

d. Supply the participants with any materials collected.

e. Make any necessary research assignments.

f. Remind the group of the time, date, and place of the actual conference.

Note: If it is impossible to arrange a preliminary meeting, the moderator will prepare items, **a, b,** and **c** and submit them to the group for approval at the actual conference.

4. Prepare an outline for the conference. This should include:

a. An introduction that:

(1) Gains the attention of the members of the group.

(2) Motivates the group to participate. (Do this as a formality, even if the group is obviously interested in the problem.)

b. A formal statement of the question.

c. Definitions of any ambiguous terms in the question.

d. The actual agenda of the meeting. This may have been determined at the preliminary meeting.

5. Remind the participants of the time, date, and place of the conference.

6. Just before the meeting, check the conference room. There should be movable chairs that can be arranged in a circle and a blackboard or easel and paper. The room should be adequately lighted and ventilated.

> The moderator has the burden of responsibility in the preliminary preparations for a conference.

The moderator's responsibilities at the conference

1. If you are the moderator, greet your fellow group members as they arrive at the meeting. See that they are comfortably seated in a face-to-face arrangement. Provide ash trays, writing materials, and name cards if needed. Sit with the group when you open the discussion. Maintain an informal attitude throughout the discussion.

2. Present your introduction and the agenda extemporaneously (that is, prepared but not memorized), in an informal, conversational style. The question itself, however, should be presented formally, exactly as worded. After defining the terms of the questions, ask for the group's acceptance of your definitions, unless this was accomplished at the preliminary meeting. If there is disagreement on the definitions, this matter should be settled before proceeding. After you state the objectives, ask for acceptance by the participants. Now, begin the discussion by asking one of the participants a question concerning the first objective or by asking for a special report, if one was assigned.

3. In conducting the discussion, apply the following suggestions:

   a. Be objective in your approach to the question. Be tactful and considerate to group members. Do not dictate to the group.

   b. Have at hand some questions that you can ask to stimulate the discussion. Use these questions when necessary.

   c. Keep the group on the objective being discussed until it has been adequately covered but follow a time schedule to prevent the discussion from bogging down on any one objective.

   d. Clarify contributions to the best of your ability, but refer points on which there is disagreement to other members of the group.

   e. See to it that all members participate. Encourage the shy members, tactfully control the overenthusiastic members, and discourage a monopoly of the discussion by one person. You can participate in the discussion, but do not take advantage of your position as moderator to overstate your own opinions or to carry a particular point.

   f. Keep a record of the main contributions made by the group. Write relevant information on the blackboard or on large sheets of paper.

   g. Make occasional summaries of the group's progress. Such summaries should certainly be made after completing each objective.

   h. Sum up the results of the discussion at the end of the meeting. Make arrangements, if necessary, for a second meeting.

The moderator's responsibilities after the conference

As soon as possible after the conference, prepare a written summary of the accomplishments and failures of the group. Send copies to the participants and other interested parties. Take any steps necessary to implement the proposed action agreed upon by the group during the conference.

In this chapter, we considered the problem-solving conference as a practical, democratic method of solving problems. We hope that you will apply these principles of discussion in your college courses and in future professional, civic, and social situations that call for use of the conference method.

The participant's responsibilities before the conference

As a member of a conference group, you will be expected to make an effective contribution to that group. Like the moderator, you will have to do some research on the problem. In some instances you may be assigned a particular research chore. If not, it is still up to you to become as informed as possible on the question.

In preparing yourself for the conference, follow these suggestions:

1. Become acquainted with the broad aspects of the problem. Try to get information on the history of the problem. What relation does the problem have to other problems? What is the nature of the problem? In this phase of your research, read from the general to the specific. For example, if the question for discussion is, "How can our community best prevent juvenile delinquency in its high schools?" you might first read from various books and periodicals dealing with the general problem of juvenile delinquency. Follow this by gathering material more specifically related to the problem in your community. This might mean getting personal interviews with high school principals and local law enforcement officers and reading anything published on the subject.

2. As you gather material on the question, be sure to record it on index cards. These information cards should then be organized according to the agenda of the conference so that your information is available when needed. In the event that an agenda has not been made available to you, use the stock objectives or develop your own agenda.

   Collect material on the subject for distribution, if available. Mark the particular references you expect to use and don't forget to bring the materials to the conference.

3. Remember that discussion is a *cooperative* search for the best solution to a problem. Keep an open mind as you do your research. Try not to form a point of view until all of the available facts have been investigated.

The participant's responsibilities during the conference

1. Be objective, courteous, and tactful throughout the conference. Avoid any type of hostility or an "I told you so" attitude.

2. Contribute to the discussion when your remarks are relevant to the issues at hand. If you have special material to report, do so when the agenda calls for it.

3. Do not monopolize the discussion. Remember that discussion implies cooperation. Give your colleagues the opportunity to state their positions and offer their contributions.

4. Be communicative when you discuss the question. All the techniques of effective communication should be used in discussion.

5. Be a good listener. This is not only a matter of courtesy, but is important to the search for a solution. Never underrate the contributions of your fellow participants.

6. If you disagree with a member of the group, express your disagreement politely and precisely. Point out the specific area of disagreement and give evidence, if available, supporting your view. If at any time you believe you are mistaken, admit it freely and proceed to the next issue.

> Be prepared to participate in the conference and participate effectively.

Projects

1. Word each of the following topics as questions for a two-hour problem-solving conference.

   a. Crime

   b. Divorce

   c. Exam cheating

   d. Civil liberties

   e. Birth control

   f. Gambling

   g. Alcholism

   h. Drug addiction

   i. School integration

   j. Air pollution

2. Using one of the above questions, as phrased for discussion, prepare an outline including the following:

   a. Introduction

   b. Statement of question for discussion

   c. Definition of terms in the question

   d. List of objectives of the conference, or agenda

   e. Motivating question on first objective

   Suggestions:

   a. Include some background material in the introduction and motivate the group to participate.

   b. List the objectives as action statements or goals of the conference: for example, "Objective Number 1: To determine the extent of juvenile delinquency in our high schools."

3. Present your prepared opening remarks to the class. Follow your outline, but use extemporaneous style (prepared but not memorized). Time: approximately two minutes.

   Suggestions:

   a. Use the blackboard to list the question and objectives.

   b. When you define the terms of the question and state the objectives, get agreement from the class on your definitions and objectives. Revise, if necessary.

4. It is suggested that for this project the instructor divide the class into groups of approximately five students each, appoint a moderator for each group, and assist the groups in selecting a suitable topic for a forty-five minute discussion period. Give each group an opportunity for a preliminary meeting (in class or out) to discuss the nature of the question, phrase the question, list the objectives, and determine areas for individual research. The preliminary meeting should take place at least one week before the conference.

Hold one conference during each class period. Allow the class time (ten to fifteen minutes) to analyze and evaluate the discussion procedures. Those members of the class not participating in the conference should offer constructive criticism of the discussion techniques used by the conference members. (See sample evaluation forms in the Appendix)

Suggested Readings

Bormann, Ernest G. and Nancy C. Bormann, *Effective Small Group Communication,* (Minneapolis: Burgess Publishing Co., 1972).

This is a brief, practical test on small group discussion. The text is divided into three parts, "The Dynamics of Good Groups," "Leadership," and "Small Group Communication."

Gully, Halbert E., *Discussion, Conference, and Group Process,* 2nd ed, (New York: Holt, Rinehart, and Winston, 1968).

Discussion, Conference, and Group Process is a well-written, well-researched text on group discussion with adequate supplementary materials on group process, language, research sources, reasoning, and interpersonal relations.

Phillips, Gerald M., *Communication and the Small Group,* (New York: Bobbs-Merrill Co., 1966).

This text is divided into five sections: "The Small Group in our Society," "Understanding the Small Group," "The Small Group in Education and Therapy," "Problem-Solving Discussion," and "Human Relations in the Small Group." It contains an adequate review of PERT (Program Evaluation and Review Techniques).

Potter, David and Martin P. Anderson, *Discussion in Small Groups: A Guide to Effective Practice,* 3rd ed. (Belmont, Cal.: Wadsworth Publishing Co., 1976).

This is a workbook with tearout pages. The text covers the structure and process of small groups, communication in small groups, and discussion techniques in small and large groups and in private and public contexts.

Rosenfeld, Lawrence B., *Human Interaction in the Small Group Setting,* (Columbus, Ohio: Bell and Howell Co., 1973).

This is an advanced text in the theory and practice of small group discussion. It lists and discusses theoretical perspectives and cites numerous research studies in the field.

Photograph by Jerald W. Rogers.

Chapter 11

Parliamentary Procedure

Performance Objectives

After studying chapter 11, you should be able to:

1. Explain the function of parliamentary procedure.
2. Cite well-known texts and authors in parliamentary procedure.
3. Define "motion," "quorum," "majority," "plurality," and "minutes."
4. List the order of business for a typical organization.
5. Demonstrate how motions are proposed by a member and acted upon by the chairperson.
6. List which motions are privileged, subsidiary, main, and incidental. Indicate for each if a second is required, if it is debatable, if it is amendable, and what vote is required for passage.
7. Explain the concept of precedence and give the order of precedence of main, subsidiary, and privileged motions.
8. List and explain seven incidental motions.
9. List the basic elements of a typical constitution and bylaws.
10. Draw up a constitution and bylaws for a hypothetical club.

WHAT IS PARLIAMENTARY PROCEDURE?

Parliamentary procedure, a term borrowed from the British, is a set of rules for conducting the meetings of democratic organizations. In some respects, parliamentary procedure is similar to the rules adopted by the United States Congress, but congressional rules, designed for a complex government body are not quite suitable for the typical club, fraternity, association, or church group. Hence, the development of a new set of rules.

Although any group may devise its own rules of procedure and state such rules in its constitution, most groups follow a similar pattern of procedural rules. Several authorities have formalized these procedures or laws in textbooks. The most notable of these is *Robert's Rules of Order* revised, first published in 1876.[1] Another widely used text, presenting a modernized version of Robert's, is the *Sturgis Standard Code of Parliamentary Procedure* (1966).[2]

THE ADVANTAGES OF USING PARLIAMENTARY PROCEDURE

Parliamentary procedure provides an orderly, systematic means of conducting business in democratic bodies. It provides for majority rule but protects minority and individual rights. As Alice Sturgis states, "Parliamentary procedure is logic and common sense crystalized into rules of law."[3]

BASIC PRINCIPLES OF PARLIAMENTARY PROCEDURE

1. The will of the majority must prevail.
2. Minority rights must be protected. That is, minorities have the right to be heard, to protest, to be allowed to present their views.
3. All members have equal rights, privileges, and obligations. All members have the right to propose motions, discuss motions fully and freely, understand the procedures being followed, be informed of the details and significance of given proposals, run for office, and nominate for office.
4. Only one question may be considered at one time. A system of motion precedence, or priority, must be observed.
5. The right of free and open discussion of all propositions must be protected.

DEFINITIONS

Majority. One more than half of the legal votes cast is a majority.

Motion. A proposed group action, stated formally by a member of a parliamentary group is called a motion. It is proposed by saying, "I move that . . ."

Plurality. The largest number of votes cast for a candidate or measure, when three or more candidates or measures are being voted upon and none has a majority, is a plurality. For example, if candidates A, B, and C are running for office and A receives five votes, B four votes, and C three votes, A has a plurality of the votes, that is, more votes than any other single candidate but less than the seven needed for a majority. In an election, a majority is required to win unless stated otherwise in the group's bylaws.

Quorum. The number of qualified members in attendance necessary to conduct the business of an organization is called a quorum. In groups with a large membership, a quorum may be only 10 percent of the total membership. If the bylaws of an organization do not state the required percentage of members necessary for a quorum, a majority of the qualified members—that is, members in good standing—is considered a quorum.

Minutes. A journal or other written record of the meeting is called the minutes of the meeting. All motions proposed, whether passed or defeated, should be recorded along with the vote. It is not necessary to include all dicussions in the minutes, only the relevant conclusions.

> Parliamentary procedure is a democratic method of conducting organizational business. It is rule by the majority with minority and individual rights.

ORDER OF BUSINESS

The order of business, or agenda, of a meeting refers to the order in which the various items of business before a group are considered. The order of business may vary slightly from one organization to another, but the following is typical:

1. Calling the meeting to order. "The meeting will please come to order."

2. Reading the minutes of the last meeting. "The secretary will please read the minutes of the last meeting." (Secretary reads minutes.) "Are there any additions or corrections?" (Pause) "If not, the minutes will stand approved as read." If there are additions or corrections, the chairperson will instruct the secretary to make the necessary changes.

3. Reports of officers and committees.

    a. Reports of officers. Example: "We will now hear the treasurer's report."

    b. Reports of standing committees.* Example: "We will now hear a report from Mr. Smith, Chairperson of the Entertainment Committee."

    c. Reports of special committees.** Example: "We will now hear a report from the Parade Committee."

4. Old business. "Is there any unfinished business?"

5. New business. "New business is now in order."

6. Announcements. "Are there any announcements?"

7. Adjournment. "If there is no further business, the Chair will entertain a motion to adjourn." After the motion is made, seconded, voted upon and passed, "The meeting is adjourned."

CLASSIFICATION OF MOTIONS

Main motions. Motions concerned with the business of the group are main motions. A main motion, can be presented by any qualified member but requires a second before it can be considered, or debated, by the group. A main motion must be disposed of before another main motion is in order.

Subsidiary motions. Motions that change or dispose of main motions are subsidiary motions. When a subsidiary motion is made in reference to a main motion, the subsidiary motion or motions must be acted upon before the main motion can be reconsidered. In other words, subsidiary motions take precedence over main motions, and have an order of precedence among themselves.

Privileged motions. Motions that are unrelated to the main motion but

*These should be read in the same order as they are listed in the bylaws.
**These should be read in order of appointment.

are important enough to take precedence over main or subsidiary motions are called privileged motions. Privileged motions are not debatable and must be acted upon before the group resumes consideration of main or subsidiary motions. For example, a motion to take a ten-minute recess is a privileged motion.

Incidental motions. Motions that arise out of other motions or have to do with procedural matters are incidental motions. Incidental motions take precedence over questions from which they arise, or, in a matter of procedure, take precedence over any new business. Incidental motions have no order of precedence among themselves, but are acted upon as they arise.

SAMPLE MOTION

MR. SMITH: (rising or raising hand) "Mr. Chairperson?"

CHAIRPERSON: "The Chair recognizes Mr. Smith."

MR. SMITH: "I move that this body send a letter of thanks to Mr. Green for his work on behalf of the club."

ANY MEMBER: "I second the motion."

CHAIRPERSON: "It has been moved and seconded to send a letter of thanks to Mr. Green for his work on behalf of the club. Is there any discussion? Mr. Smith." (It is customary to give the maker of a motion the first opportunity to discuss the question.)

(General Discussion) If there is no further discussion, we will proceed to the vote. All in favor of the motion to send a letter of thanks to Mr. Green for his work on behalf of the club, say "Aye!" (Response) "All opposed, say, "No!" (Chairperson judges response.) "The 'Ayes' have it and the motion is carried. Is there any other new business?" (If the voice vote is close, the Chairperson may ask for a show of hands or a standing vote that is counted by the secretary and reported to the Chairperson. Or, if the question is controversial, the Chairperson may first ask for a show of hands or a standing vote.)

How to make a motion

1. Members who want to make a motion must first gain recognition from the chairperson. They may do this by standing or raising their

hands, as custom dictates, and calling, "Mr. Chairperson" (or "Madam Chairperson," if appropriate).

2. Any member may second a motion without receiving recognition.

3. The chairperson should repeat the motion after it has been seconded and before it is discussed. The motion should be repeated when put to a vote.

4. In informal groups, it is often the custom to briefly explain a motion before proposing it. In more formal groups, such an explanation is usually typed and given to the members before the meeting.

Table 11–1 summarizes the rules pertaining to the different kinds of motions.

MAIN MOTIONS

General main motion. A proposal for some action on the part of the organization is a general main motion. Main motions have to do with the usual business of the group. Any member, after gaining recognition can say: "I move that this body send a letter of appreciation to Mr. Green for his work on behalf of this club."

Specific main motions

Reconsider. To set aside some previous action of the group and resume consideration of the proposal as though no vote had been taken is to reconsider a motion. This applies to main motions and motions to amend. A motion may only be reconsidered during the current meeting. If no other business is pending; that is, still being considered, the motion to reconsider is taken up immediately. If other business has to be decided, that business is concluded and then the motion to reconsider is taken up. Any member, without recognition from the chair, can say: "I move to reconsider the vote to raise our club dues passed earlier." Some parliamentarians insist that the maker of the motion to reconsider must have voted on the winning side of the question in dispute.

Rescind. To overturn a main motion previously passed is to rescind the motion. A motion to rescind can be made at any time when a main mo-

TABLE 11–1. Table of Motions.

Precedence of Motions (from highest to lowest)	Second Re- quired?	De- bat- able?	Amend- able?	Vote Re- quired	May Inter- rupt
Privileged Motions					
To fix time and place of next meeting	yes	no	yes*	majority	no
To adjourn	yes	no	no	majority	no
To take a recess **	yes	no	yes†	majority	no
Question of privilege	no	no	no	none	yes
Subsidiary Motions					
Lay on the table	yes	no	no	majority	no
Previous question††	yes	no	no	$2/3$ majority	no
Limit debate	yes	no	yes	$2/3$ majority	no
Postpone definitely	yes	yes	yes	majority	no
Refer to committee	yes	yes	yes	majority	no
Amend	yes	yes	yes	majority	no
Postpone indefinitely	yes	yes	no	majority	no
Main Motions					
General main motion	yes	yes	yes	majority	no
Specific main motion					
Reconsider	yes	yes	no	majority	yes
Rescind	yes	yes	no	majority‡	no
Take from table	yes	no	no	majority	no
Incidental Motions					
Appeal decision	yes	yes	no	tie vote	yes
Point of order	no	no	no	none	yes
Parliamentary inquiry	no	no	no	none	yes
Withdraw a motion	no	no	no	none	no
Object to consider	no	no	no	$2/3$ opposed	yes
Suspend rules	yes	no	no	$2/3$ majority	no
Division of question	no	no	no	none	no
Division of assembly	no	no	no	none	yes

*Time and place may be amended.
†Time may be amended.
**Are considered main motions when no other motions are pending.
††A motion to stop debate and vote immediately.
‡Requires $2/3$ majority unless otherwise announced before the meeting.

tion would be in order. It applies to decisions made at any previous meeting. Rescinding, however, cannot undo action already undertaken as a result of a passed motion. Any member, after gaining recognition, can say: "I move to rescind the motion passed at our last meeting by which this organization agreed to send a letter of appreciation to Mr. Green for his work on behalf of this club." This would not be in order if the letter had already been mailed.

Take from the table. To resume consideration of a motion previously tabled is called taking from the table. Such a motion is in order any time after other business has been taken care of. Taking from the table takes precedence over other new main motions. Any member can say: "I move to take from the table the motion to paint our clubhouse."

SUBSIDIARY MOTIONS

Postpone indefinitely. The question being considered can be suppressed or killed by being postponed indefinitely. This applies to main motions only. Motions to postpone indefinitely are used as test votes to see how members stand on the main motion. Any member can say: "I move that the motion before the assembly be postponed indefinitely."

Amend. To alter or perfect a main motion is to amend it. Amendments may be made by striking out words, adding words, substituting words (called strike out and insert), or by substituting an entire new motion that is relevant to the intent of the original motion. There are two ranks of amendments, first and second. The first rank applies to amending the main motion; the second, to amending an amendment. There can be only one amendment of each rank awaiting a vote at any one time. For example, the main motion is, "I move that we paint our clubhouse." The amendment of the first rank is, "I move to amend the motion by adding the word *green* after the word *clubhouse*." The amendment of the second rank is, "I move to amend the amendment by striking the word *green* and inserting the word *blue*."

In our example, in which there are obviously many other colors to choose from, the chairperson may "create a blank" to replace *green*, thus allowing other colors to be voted upon as follows: "If there are no objections, the color of paint will be considered a blank, so that all colors may be considered." Any color then suggested is listed and, when the list is compiled, each color is voted upon.

Refer to committee. To allow investigation or further study of a problem by a small group, a motion may be referred to committee. Any member can say: "I move to refer the picnic question to the Entertainment Committee for study and recommendation."

Postpone definitely. To delay a vote on a motion to a particular time in order to allow further study of the proposal is to postpone definitely. Any member can say: "I move to postpone consideration of the motion until our next meeting."

Limit debate. To speed up the business of the assembly, the members can limit debate. Since this is an abridgement of freedom of speech, a two-thirds affirmative vote is required for passage. Any member can say: "I move to limit debate on this question to ten minutes."

Previous question. A motion of previous question cuts off debate and forces an immediate vote on the undecided question (or on all undecided questions). A motion of previous question requires a two-thirds vote for passage. Any member can say: "I move the previous question." Or, "I move the previous question on all pending questions."

Lay on the table. To lay a motion on the table is to postpone it temporarily. This gives members more time to consider the question. A motion may be taken from the table after any change in business. In actual use, this motion is often used as a delaying tactic to "kill" a motion. Any member can say: "I move to lay the motion on the table."

PRIVILEGED MOTIONS

Question of privilege. A motion of question of privilege is used to secure immediate action concerning the comforts or rights of the members. It is not a motion in the true sense, since the question is settled by the chairperson. Any member can say, without recognition: "Mr. Chairperson, I rise to a question of privilege."

To take a recess. A motion to take a recess is used to allow a few minutes of relaxation in a long session or to allow time to prepare matters for the assembly. The motion can be amended as to the length of time of the recess. Any member can say: "I move that we take a recess of fifteen minutes."

To adjourn. A motion to adjourn is used to terminate the meeting. Unless the time and place of a following meeting has been established, the motion to adjourn has the effect of dissolving the organization. Any member can say: "I move to adjourn." A *qualified* motion to adjourn ("I move that we adjourn *at five o'clock"*) is a main motion and is treated as such.

To fix the time and place of the next meeting. Motions to fix time and place provide for a continuation of meetings of the group. They are especially important when no regular meetings have been scheduled. Such motions take precedence over all other motions. Any member can say: "I move that we adjourn and reconvene (reassemble) at 7 P.M. next Wednesday in this hall." or "I move that, when we adjourn, we reassemble at 7 P.M. next Wednesday in this hall."

INCIDENTAL MOTIONS

Appeal decision from the chair. A motion to appeal decision is used to object to a ruling of the chairperson. Any member, without recognition, can say: "Mr. Chairperson, I appeal the decision from the Chair." After the motion is seconded, the chairperson says: "Will you state the grounds for your objection?" Following discussion, the motion is put to the group in the affirmative: "Those in favor of sustaining the decision of the Chair, say 'Aye.'" (A tie vote sustains the Chair.)

Point of order. A motion of point of order is used to correct an error in procedure. Any member, without recognition, can say: "Mr. Chairperson, I rise to a point of order." Then the chairperson says: "State your point of order." The member points out the error. The chairperson, agreeing with the member, says: "Your point of order is well taken; the motion to . . . is out of order." Or, disagreeing, "Your point of order is not well taken; is there any further discussion?"

Parliamentary inquiry. To obtain information from the presiding officer on a procedural matter a motion of parliamentary inquiry is used. A member proposing such a motion may interrupt a speaker. Any member, without recognition, can say: "I rise to a parliamentary inquiry." Then the chairperson says: "State you inquiry."

Withdraw a motion. Withdrawing a motion enables members, upon changing their minds, to remove their motions from consideration. If the motion has not been restated by the chairperson, the proposer simply states: "I withdraw my motion." If the motion has been restated by the chairperson, the proposer may say: "I request permission to withdraw my motion." Then the chairperson says: "If there are no objections, the motion may be withdrawn." If there are objections, the motion must be considered.

Object to consideration. A motion to object to consideration is used to avoid considering or discussing a question that is unsuitable for any reason. Any member, without recognition, can say: "Mr. Chairperson, I object to the consideration of this question." The Chairperson, without waiting for a second, then says: "Those in favor of considering the question, please rise." A two-thirds vote *against* consideration is needed to avoid discussion.

Division of question. Division of question is proposed to allow members to consider the parts of a complex question separately. Any member, upon gaining recognition, can say: "I request that the question be divided as follows . . . " The chairperson, if he or she concurs, divides the question as proposed.

Division of assembly. Division of assembly is used to verify a doubtful voice vote. Any member, without recognition, can say: "I call for division." The chairperson will immediately ask for a standing vote or a show of hands. The vote will be tabulated and announced to the assembly.

KEEPING THE MINUTES OF A MEETING

The minutes of a meeting are taken by the secretary of the group. They are a careful record of business carried on by the organization or a committee of the organization.

The first paragraph of the minutes of a meeting should state the kind of meeting (regular or special), the name of the organization, the time, date, and place when the meeting was called to order, and the name of the presiding officer.

The body of the minutes should contain a record of motions and reports made (and by whom), and the action taken. A tabulation of votes, when other than voice votes should be included. No record should be made of actual discussion, nor should personal comment and opinion be included. After the meeting, the minutes should be typed.

At the beginning of each meeting, the minutes of the last meeting are usually read by the secretary. After the reading, the chairperson will ask for corrections or additions. If there are no changes to be made the chairperson will state: "If there are no additions or corrections, the minutes will stand approved as read." The secretary will write "approved" at the end of the minutes and date and sign them.

THE CONSTITUTION AND BYLAWS OF AN ORGANIZATION

The constitution of an organization contains the basic rules governing the organization. The bylaws are an extension of the constitution. They state more complete details on the provisions of the constitution.

Basic elements of a constitution

Preamble: An introductory statement about the general purpose and nature of the organization.
Article 1:   Name of the organization.
Article 2:   Purpose of the organization.
Article 3:   Qualifications for membership.
Article 4:   Officers required for the organization.
Article 5   Provisions for a governing board or directors.
Article 6:   Time and place for regular meetings and provisions for calling special meetings.
Article 7:   Number of members constituting a quorum.
Article 8:   Method of amending the constitution.

Basic elements of the bylaws

1. Membership. Kinds of members, method of selecting them, and their duties and rights; limitations on their number, and method of terminating membership.
2. Committees. Standing committees, method of selecting committee members, duties and powers of committees, time of meetings, quorum requirements.
3. Financing. Dues, fines, initiation fees, debt limits.
4. Officers. Number and titles of officers, their duties, terms; method of selecting them.
5. Meetings. Time and place of regular meetings, method of calling special meetings, notice requirements.
6. Order of business.
7. Parliamentary rules. (Specify authority, for example *Robert's Rules*.)
8. Procedure for amending the constitution and bylaws.
9. Quorum requirements.
10. Conventions.

Projects

1. Practice in making and acting upon motions. (It is suggested that the instructor act as chairperson at first.)

   a. List four motions, in order of precedence, on the blackboard, as we have done in the table below.

Motion	Second required?	Debat-able?	Amend-able?	Vote required
Refer to committee	Yes	Yes	Yes	Majority
Amend	Yes	Yes	Yes	Majority
Postpone indefinitely	Yes	Yes	No	Majority
Main motion	Yes	Yes	Yes	Majority

   b. Suggest a name for a hypothetical club, for example; "The College Speech Club." Appoint a temporary secretary to take minutes.

   c. Only the motions listed by the instructor may be used in practice. Ask a member of the class to make a main motion pertaining to the business of the club. Ask for a second. Proceed with practice in stating and acting upon motions. In order to learn the motions and rules rapidly, it is suggested that discussion be curtailed and that each member, in alphabetical order, advance the main motion by applying to it one of the subsidiary motions. As the class gains practice in making and disposing of motions, additional motions may be added. Also, students may be rotated as chairpersons. The instructor will explain motions, precedence, and so forth, as new motions are added.

2. The chairperson calls the club to order and asks the secretary to read the minutes, and so on. When new business is reached on the agenda, continue practice in making motions as in Project 1.

3. Appoint a temporary chairperson. Announce that temporary officers will be elected. The temporary chairperson will proceed with nominations and elections.

4. List the outlines of a constitution and bylaws on the blackboard. The group, using parliamentary procedure, should develop the constitution and vote upon it. It may be desirable to assign committees to develop sections of the bylaws in a similar fashion and to report back to the main body for further action on each contribution.

$\mathcal{N}$otes

1. Henry M. Robert, *Robert's Rules of Order Revised* (New York: Scott, Foresman, and Company, 1915)
2. Alice F. Sturgis, *Sturgis Standard Code of Parliamentary Procedure* (New York: McGraw-Hill Book Co., Inc., 1951)
3. Alice F.Sturgis, *Learning Parliamentary Procedure* (New York: McGraw-Hill Book Co. Inc., 1953) p. 15

Suggested Readings

Gray, John W. and Richard G. Rea, *Parliamentary Procedure: A Programmed Introduction*, (Glenview, Ill.: Scott, Foresman & Co., 1963).

A programmed text on parliamentary procedure, this book is written for self-learning. It is presented in a clear, easy-to-read style.

Hellman, Hugo E., *Parliamentary Procedure*, (New York: MacMillan Co., 1966).

A paperback text on the basic motions and procedures in parliamentary law.

Robert, Henry M. et al, *Robert's Rules of Order Newly Revised*, (Glenview, Ill.: Scott, Foresman & Co., 1970).

An updated, modern version of the earlier editions.

Sturgis, Alice F., *Learning Parliamentary Procedure*, (New York: McGraw-Hill Book Co., 1953).

Sturgis is also the author of *Sturgis' Standard Code of Parliamentary Procedure* (1966), a more detailed, technical approach to the subject. Both texts are quite popular, especially on college campuses.

Wagner, Joseph A., *Successful Leadership in Groups and Organizations*, 2nd ed., (San Francisco: Chandler Pub. Co., 1973).

A short but good presentation of parliamentary procedure and group discussion, this book is suitable for a short, combination course in group discussion and parliamentary procedure.

Part Three

Public
Speaking

UNACCUSTOMED AS I AM
TO PUBLIC SPEAKING...

Chapter 12

Planning Your Speech

Performance Objectives

After studying chapter 12, you should be able to:

1. Explain the three recommended methods of speech presentation.
2. Define extemporaneous speaking.
3. List and explain the four general purposes of public speaking.
4. List and explain the seven key steps in preparing a speech.
5. List and discuss the three general sources of speech materials.
6. Prepare a typical four-by-six inch note card labeled with general topic, specific topic, bibliography, and research data.
7. Explain the difference between a preliminary outline, a working outline, and a speaking outline.
8. Explain how one should practice an extemporaneous speech.

Photograph by Jerald W. Rogers.

So you're going to give a speech! When? Where? To whom? Why? All of these questions are important and must be carefully answered if your speech is to be successful. But before we get too involved with these questions, let's be sure we agree on the nature of public speaking. What is public speaking? How is a speech presented? Why do we give a speech?

THE NATURE OF PUBLIC SPEAKING

Public speaking is an oral communication in which one person presents, in some detail, his or her thoughts and feelings on a subject to a group of listeners. Public speaking always has a definite purpose. In most cases, speakers will plan and prepare their talks in advance. And usually speakers deliver their talks facing their listeners, who may be seated or standing in a formal gathering.

Methods of delivering a speech

There are four possible methods of presenting a talk: (1) impromptu, (2) reading from manuscript, (3) extemporaneous, and (4) memorized. However, since memorization is a difficult method of delivery, it is not recommended in this text. Instead, we prefer the other three types of presentation.

Impromptu. An impromptu speech is one that is entirely unprepared. This method of delivery is often referred to as "speaking off the cuff" or "on the spur of the moment." You will find it necessary to be adept at this type of speaking at business meetings, conferences, dinners, political rallies, or social gatherings.

Reading from manuscript. You may sometimes find it advisable to write out your speech and read from it. For example, some political or governmental speeches are so important that the speaker does not want to depend on extemporaneous delivery. The disadvantage of this type of presentation is that the speech usually sounds read, or 'read-y,' as it is called in radio language. With training and practice, however, you can avoid the read-y quality and become an able speech reader.

Extemporaneous. The extemporaneous speech is thoroughly prepared and rehearsed but not memorized. It is the most popular method of speech presentation today and is the method that will be emphasized throughout this book. When you give an extemporaneous talk, it is assumed that you will plan your talk well in advance of the speaking date. You will know your time allowance, the occasion for the speech, and the kind of audience to expect. You will have selected a suitable subject, know your speech purpose, and have thoroughly researched the topic to the best of your ability. You will have organized and outlined your speech materials and have rehearsed the speech and prepared some speaking notes if they are needed. This is what is meant by an extemporaneous speech.

> The recommended methods of delivery are: impromptu, reading from a manuscript, and extemporaneous.

PURPOSES OF PUBLIC SPEAKING

When you give a talk to a group of people, you should have a reason for doing so. You should not talk to show off or to kill time. All public speaking should be purposive; that is, you should know exactly what you expect to accomplish by speaking to a group.

The majority of speeches can be classified by purpose under four general headings:

1. *To inform.* When you wish to instruct, enlighten, clarify, or explain, your purpose is to inform. Many speeches fall into this category; the teacher's lecture, the foreman's instructions, the scientist's explanation of a process. Much of our education is received through the speech to inform.

2. *To entertain.* Speeches to entertain are intended to amuse or interest the listeners. The entertainment speech is often humorous, satirical, or a light treatment of a serious topic. Social functions, such as banquets, are typical situations for an entertaining after-dinner speech.

3. *To strengthen belief.* When your aim is to reinforce existing values, attitudes, or beliefs; or when you wish to inspire, stimulate, or urge your listeners to action, you give a speech to strengthen belief. An important requirement of a successful speech to strengthen belief is that the audience must already believe or approve of your basic contention or your point of view. Speeches to strengthen belief are heard at graduation exercises, pep rallies, political conventions, and religious gatherings, among others.

4. *To change belief.* When you want to convince or persuade an audience to accept an attitude, belief, or course of action to which they are indifferent or hostile, your purpose will be to change belief. Your speech, in this instance, is aimed at those members of your audience who are negative or neutral toward the subject or contention being presented.

Students of public speaking often misunderstand the divisions of speech goals or purposes, since many of the purposes seem to overlap. For example, in a speech to change belief, you will probably give some factual information (to inform), you may wish to arouse or inspire your audience (to strengthen belief), and you may even wish to include some humor in your speech (to entertain). But these three "purposes" are only devices to achieve your real goal—to change belief. When planning your speech, always think in terms of your final goal—the reaction you wish to obtain from you audience.

The general purposes of public speaking are:

To inform,

To entertain,

To strengthen belief and/or to actuate, and

To change belief and/or to actuate.

The specific purpose of your speech

In planning your speech, it is not enough to know the general purpose of the speech. You should also know the specific purpose of your talk—what, exactly, you want your audience to know or do. How do you want them to react? In your planning, always include the specific purpose as well as the general purpose. For example, in a speech on tennis (general purpose to inform) your specific purpose may be to explain to the audience how to deliver a good serve.

WHAT ABOUT STAGE FRIGHT?

Experiencing so-called stage fright in public speaking should not give you much alarm. Most speakers experience some degree of nervousness before and during a speech. In fact, some tenseness is desirable. It gives vitality and life to the speech. There are however, some positive steps that you can take to reduce stage fright. You can *know* your subject. You can practice your presentation thoroughly. You can gain experience by speaking often.

> To combat stage fright, realize that some nervous tension is desirable. Know your subject and practice adequately. Speak publicly as often as possible.

KEY STEPS IN PLANNING YOUR SPEECH

1. Analyze the occasion.
2. Analyze the audience.
3. Select and narrow the subject.
4. Determine your purpose.
5. Gather material.
6. Outline the speech.
7. Practice the speech.

Analyze the occasion

When is the speech to be given—both time and date? Where is the meeting to be held—the address and room number? Who is sponsoring the meeting—who is the chairperson? What is the purpose of the meeting? What is the program for the meeting? Are other speakers involved? What are the time limits for your talk? What are the facilities of the meeting room? Is a lectern furnished? A microphone? A blackboard?

Most of these questions are obvious, but they are all important and should be answered before the speech is given. If possible, visit the meeting place in advance to observe first hand the facilities available.

Analyze the audience

Find out, if possible, the make-up of your expected audience. Does it consist of adults, young people, children, or a mixed group? What is the percentage of men and women, boys and girls? What is the educational, vocational, and economic background of the audience? Do the members have any special interests as a group? Can you predict any attitudes, prejudices, or political leanings that might be held by many members of the group?

The make-up and characteristics of your audience will be very important to you in the selection of your topic, your purpose, and the type of material included in your talk. Obviously you would not give the same talk to a group of parents and teachers that you would give to a troop of Boy Scouts.

Select and narrow the subject

Choose a subject of interest to *you* and about which you have or can obtain special knowledge. For example, the mayor of a certain community gave a talk on local government. The speech was both interesting and informative because the speaker was talking about a subject that interested him and about which he had special knowledge.

Choose a subject that suits the occasion.

Choose a subject that you think would be of concern or interest to your audience.

Choose a subject, or aspect of a subject, that can be covered in the time given to you. You cannot very well give a speech on the Russian Revolution if you are limited to five minutes.

As a final test of your choice of a speech subject answer the following question. If you can answer it well, you are on the right track: Why this subject to this audience at this time on this occasion?

Determine your purpose

After you have selected and narrowed your subject, it is important that you determine the purpose of your speech. You should know your general and specific purposes and the audience reaction to expect. For example, let's assume that the title of your speech is "Checkmate." Your general purpose is probably to inform. Your specific purpose might be to explain the moves of the chess pieces. The expected audience reaction would probably be one of understanding.

Gather material

When you have decided on the subject and purpose, you are ready to gather material for you speech. There are three general sources of material: (1) Personal experience and knowledge; (2) Experience and knowledge of others, which can be obtained by interviewing others, listening to lectures, and so on; and (3) Written sources.

1. *Personal experience and knowledge.* When planning your talk, the first thing to do is to draw upon your own experience and knowledge for speech material. What do you already know about the subject? What have you read or studied that would apply to the subject? Would this data be suitable to the purpose of your talk?

   A word of warning at this point: Do not trust your memory. Jot down your ideas on cards. You will want to prepare a preliminary outline later.

2. *Experience and knowledge of others.* Talk about your proposed speech with other people. Get the ideas of members of your family and friends. For specific, authoritative information you may wish to arrange an interview with some expert in the field. Other sources of information are lectures and material from radio, television, the theater, and similar types of mass-media communication. Again, be sure to take notes in every instance! Your notes should be documented, indicating the speaker, subject, date, and occasion.

3. *Written sources.* The most important source of material for speeches of any degree of complexity is the vast accumulation of printed works, including books, newspapers, and periodicals. Usually this type of information is readily available to all. Aside from the periodicals and newspapers that most of us buy, the library provides all kinds of publications. It is up to *you* to know your library. You should know how to look up material on any subject. You should familiarize yourself with the card catalogue, indexes, and the reference books available.

In summary, you can get material for your speech from three sources: your personal experience and knowledge, what others tell you of their experience and knowledge, and printed matter. The complexity of your subject will determine how many sources you will need in gathering material for your speech. Sometimes your own experience and knowledge may be sufficient. For example, if you were a tennis player giving a talk on how to play tennis, you might depend entirely upon your own experience and knowledge for the materials of your speech. In other instances, however, it may be necessary to draw upon the other two general sources of information. At no time will you exhaust the sources of material. In most cases you will be limited by time in your research task, but if you have done a good job of recording and documenting your findings you will gradually develop a fund of valuable information that you can use in future speeches.

> When researching for a speech, don't trust your memory. Take notes, quoting or paraphrasing, and be sure to document them with author, title, source, and date.

What type of notes should be taken on speech source materials?

Use a card system in recording items for your speech. In addition to the actual quotes or paraphrased material that you want to remember, each card should indicate the general subject, the specific subject, the author, title, publisher, date, and page numbers quoted from. If you are taking notes from an oral rather than a printed source, your card should indicate the speaker, subject, date, and occasion. Figure 12–1 is an example of a typical research notation on a four-by-six inch card.

Note that the general subject is indicated in the upper right-hand corner, the specific subject in the upper left-hand corner, and the source data on the second line. The quoted material is then recorded and may be carried over to additional cards if needed. If this is the case, the supplementary cards should be lettered 1–a, 1–b, and so on, and should contain the general and specific subject titles and the author and title but not the other source data.

The Supreme Court   Crime

"The Law," Time, July 19, 1976, p. 43.
    "The Supreme Court often winds up issuing one of its most important decisions on the concluding day of the term. Last week was no exception. Just before hanging up their robes for a badly needed summer recess—the 39-week term was among the longest ever—the Justices issued a ruling that means an end to almost all review by federal courts of alleged violations by states of the Fourth Amendment search and seizure provisions."

FIGURE 12–1.
Research notation.

Outline the speech

There are three types of outline that you will find useful in preparing your talk: the *prelimanary outline*, the *working outline*, and the *speaking outline*.

The *preliminary outline* serves to narrow your topic, suggests the major divisions of your speech, and serves as a guide in your research. This outline should contain the title, the purpose, the major points that you expect to cover, and any specific facts or personal experiences that might be used in the speech. Let us assume that you wish to give a talk on chess. Your preliminary outline might look something like the following:

TITLE (OPTIONAL):   Checkmate
GENERAL PURPOSE: To inform
SPECIFIC PURPOSE: To teach the audience how to play chess. Expected
                    audience reaction: understanding.

I. Introduction
  A. Gain attention (and indicate topic)
  B. Motivate audience to listen
  C. Give purpose sentence
II. Body
  A. The names and positions of the pieces
  B. The prescribed moves of the pieces
  C. Procedure in playing the game
III. Conclusion

Note that the outline is incomplete, but that it acts as a guide in the further preparation of your speech. You have decided that you will probably cover three major points in the body of your talk. These subdivisions now guide you in gathering material. It is up to you to research the areas indicated by your three major points and to include the information in your working outline.

Your *working outline* will fill in the details of the preliminary outline, after the necessary research on the topic has been done. It will contain the material of the preliminary outline, further developed, and a complete introduction and conclusion.

Your working outline should contain much more material than you will actually use in your speech. Better too much than too little.

Sample Working Outline

Checkmate

II. Body
  A. The names and positions of the pieces in order of importance. Each player has the following pieces (show positions on blackboard):
    1. There are eight pawns.
    2. There are two knights.
    3. There are two bishops.
    4. There are two rooks.
    5. There is one queen.
    6. There is one king.
  B. Moves of the various pieces.
    1. Pawns may only move forward. They may move just one space at a time, except for their first move, when they may move one or two spaces. Pawns may move one space forward diagonally to capture an opposing piece.
    2. Knights may move in any direction as follows: One space vertically or horizontally, then one space diagonally forward in the same general direction. Knights may jump over any chess piece, friendly or unfriendly.
    3. Bishops may move diagonally in any direction as many spaces as are free; that is, not containing a chess piece.
    4. Rooks may move horizontally or vertically as many spaces as are free.
    5. The queen may move in any direction for as many spaces as are free.
    6. The king may move one space in any direction unless such a move would place him in a check position.
  C. Playing the game.
    1. The purpose of the game is to place the opponent's king in check; that is, in a position in which he can be captured.
    2. If the opponent's king is in check and he cannot move it out of check, your opponent has lost the game. This is checkmate.
    3. In order to place the opponent's king in check, it is advisable to take as many of the opponent's pieces as possible in the early stages of the game.

Next, prepare the introduction and conclusion. For example:

I. Introduction
   A. Gain attention: Here's a wargame in which no one gets hurt. It's called chess and it is a game of skill.
   B. Motivation: We all enjoy a good game. And we all need to relax after a tiring school day. So I am sure that you will enjoy the game of chess.
   C. Purpose sentence: I am going to explain the game of chess. Let me first draw a picture of the chess board.

II. Conclusion
   I have described for you the essentials of chess, beginning with a description of the pieces, their positions on the board, and their various moves. May I suggest that all of you take up this fascinating game. You will certainly enjoy it.

Rearrange your outline in logical order—introduction, body, and conclusion. Now, let us consider your speaking outline or notes—if you need them at all. The speaking outline should be very brief, possibly a skeleton outline on three-by-five inch cards so that your notes can be as inconspicuous as possible.

Sample speaking outline

Card 1. Chess is a wargame but no one gets hurt.
Card 2. Chess is fun, good relaxation.
Card 3. Describe the pieces and placement on board.
Card 4. (Draw board on blackboard)
Card 5. Moves of the pieces.
Card 6. Purpose of the game.
Card 7. Take up chess for fun, excitement, and relaxation.

Suggestions for outlining

1. Use a three-part outline including the introduction, body, and conclusion. Prepare the body of your outline first, and then the introduction and conclusion. Rearrange the parts in the normal order.

2. Use a system of letters, numerals, and indentations to show the relationship of items in the outline. For example:

II. Body
   A. Major statement
      1. Supporting statement
      2. Supporting statement
         a. Sub-support
         b. Sub-support
   B. Second major statement

3. Each item in your outline should be self-explanatory. Use complete thoughts but in abbreviated form. However, you may wish to write out the introduction.

4. Your outline should be impersonal. Avoid personal pronouns, except in the introduction.

5. Cite the source of your material after the item concerned, to be used in your speech as you think best.

6. To supplement your outline, prepare a bibliography of the materials you used.

Practice the speech

After you have prepared your working outline, practice giving your speech using the outline. Time yourself. Spend more or less time on items as needed. Check for time once more. Then prepare your skeleton outline, or speaking notes. Put these notes on three-by-five inch cards. Go over your speech a third time, using your notes when necessary. During this practice and those that follow, give the speech exactly as you plan to deliver it. Stand, use gestures, move about, and so on. You are now ready to try out your speech on a test audience such as a friend or a member of your family. Ask your listeners for criticism. Did they understand your ideas? Did they understand your purpose?

Now make any final changes in your talk. Indicate the changes in your notes and rehearse the revised speech once more. You are now ready to present your speech to your intended audience. Good luck!

SUGGESTED SUBJECT AREAS

To inform

1. How to play: football, baseball, basketball, tennis, golf, badminton, lacrosse, table tennis, shuffleboard, croquet, quoits, horseshoes, darts, bridge, canasta, chess, checkers.
2. How to: swim, dive, sail a boat, ride a horse, fish, dance, exercise, fly a kite, play a musical instrument, plan a budget.
3. How to build: a birdhouse, a divider, a planter, a bookcase, a boat, a model ship, a go-cart, a bar, a rock garden.
4. How to: study, read a book, be a good conversationalist, make friends, apply makeup, give a home permanent, make a dress.
5. Handcrafts: jewelry, leatherwork, copper, beads, weaving.
6. Hobbies: flower arrangement, tropical fish, hi-fi, short-wave radio, stamp collecting, coin collecting, model cars.

Practicing speaking. (Courtesy of New York University.)

To strengthen belief

1. Social topics: Crime doesn't pay; Be a good neighbor; Drive carefully; Contribute to your favorite charity; Go to the polls and vote; Take an active part in local government; Don't be a litter bug; The value of education; Help the undereprivileged; Stop air and water pollution; Join the club.

2. Personal topics; Take care of your health; Eat a well-balanced diet; Exercise regularly; Watch your manners; Give up smoking; Dress appropriately; Keep in touch with friends; Read more.

3. Patriotic topics: Be glad you're an American; Freedom is important; Democracy is the best form of government; Communism must be stopped; Equal rights for all; Preserve free speech.

4. Inspirational topics:
   a. Biographical: Speeches on famous persons.
   b. General: Ethics, morals, courage, love, friendship, duty, fidelity, family unity, patriotism, religion, teamwork.

To change belief

1. Social topics: Capital punishment; Civil rights; Divorce; Sex education; Birth control; Abortion; Prostitution; Gambling; Juvenile delinquency; Crime; Narcotics; Alcohol; Euthenasia; Vivisection; Medicare; Poverty programs.

2. Political topics: Foreign policy; The United Nations; Communist China; Cuba; Political parties; Urban renewal; Space program; Air pollution, Federal Health Program; Tax reform.

To entertain

1. The speech to entertain may be a light treatment of the serious topics already mentioned. Such treatment may often involve the use of satire, exaggeration, and humor.

2. General: Interesting personalities; Marital relations; Pets; Children; Professional caricatures; Political caricatures; Travel; Unusual experiences; Different customs.

Projects

1. Prepare a preliminary outline on a speech topic of your choice. Indicate the general purpose, the specific purpose, and the expected audience reaction.
2. Develop the speech introduction outline for the same subject. Did you include the attention step, the motivation step, and the purpose sentence?
3. Assume that you are to give a talk to the local P.T.A. Complete the Occasion and Audience Analysis form in the Appendix for an imaginary speech at the P.T.A.'s monthly meeting.
4. List three potential subjects for each of the four speech types (to inform, to strengthen belief, to change belief, and to entertain). Be as specific as possible.

Suggested Readings

Monroe, Alan and Douglas Ehninger, *Principles of Speech Communication*, 7th brief ed., (Glenview, Ill.; Scott, Foresman & Co., 1975). See Chap. 3, "Planning and Preparing the Speech."

Verderber, Rudolph F., *The Challenge of Effective Speaking*, 3rd ed., (Belmont, Cal.: Wadsworth Publishing Co., 1976). See Chap. 4, "Organizing Speech Materials."

Chapter 13

Developing Your Speech

Performance Objectives

After studying chapter 13, you should be able to:

1. List and explain patterns of organizing a speech.
2. List and explain eight *speech supports,* the verbal and audio-visual devices that give "body" to a speech.
3. List and explain five verbal devices that can be used to reinforce or emphasize a particular point in a speech.
4. Explain the three parts of the speech introduction.
   a. List and illustrate six methods of gaining attention.
   b. Explain the function of the motivation step.
   c. Explain and illustrate the purpose sentence.
5. Explain "Borden's Formula."
6. Describe three methods of concluding a speech.
7. List six suggestions for wording a speech, and explain the difference between oral and written discourse.

Photograph by Jerald W. Rogers.

ORGANIZING THE SPEECH

Suppose you wanted to give a talk about your automobile trip across the country. What would you first describe to your audience: the beauty of the Grand Canyon, the bears in Yellowstone National Park, or the wonders of Mammoth Cave? Or, perhaps you could relate your day-by-day experiences—what you saw the first day, where you visited the second day, and so on. Most subjects can be organized according to a definite pattern and it is up to you to select the pattern that will be best for your purposes. This process is called *organizing the speech.*

We have already mentioned the standard division of a speech into three parts: the introduction, body, and conclusion. Let's now consider the order of the subject matter within the body of the speech.

Some of the more common patterns used in speeches are chronological order, space order, topical order, causal order, and problem-solution order.

Chronological order. Many subjects lend themselves to organization by time sequence. "How To Do It" speeches almost invariably follow a chronological order. For example, if you give a talk on "How to change a tire" you will probably follow a time pattern and say something like, "First you brake the car, then you remove the jack from the trunk . . . ." You are following a time sequence or chronological order. Speeches dealing with historical events, personal experiences and biographies may also be developed chronologically.

Space order. Some topics can best be developed using a space pattern; that is, left to right, top to bottom, east to west. A speech describing a home or building might use space order organization to discuss the first floor, second floor, and so on. In your imaginary speech describing your cross-country trip, perhaps space order organization would be desirable. You could organize your speech by state or by tourist attraction, both examples of space order.

Topical order. Some subjects are usually divided by topic. For example, the subject of taxation may be considered from the point of view of local, state, and federal taxation. Government may be divided into the executive, legislative, and judicial branches. Topical organization applies only to the division of a subject and not to the order in which topics are presented. This is up to the speaker. One method of topical order is climactic; that is, beginning with a topic of lesser importance and ending with the topic of greatest importance.

Causal order. Sometimes a speech can best be organized by cause to effect, or effect to cause relationship. For example, a speech on crime might best be developed by discussing the various causes of crime or by showing how minor offenses lead to major crimes.

Problem-solution order. Problem-solution order is usually used in persuasive speeches and debate presentations. The speaker tries to prove that a problem confronts us and offers a desirable solution to that problem. Topics such as Juvenile delinquency, Divorce, Gambling, War, Civil rights, and Gun control laws can usually best be developed using a problem-solution order.

Although some speech subjects can easily be organized according to a particular pattern, other speeches are more difficult to analyze and divide. It is up to you to carefully study your speech subject and purpose and then divide the subject into its logical parts and decide in what order to present them.

> Your speech should be organized according to a pattern that is logical and appropriate to your speech purpose.

DEVELOPING THE BODY OF YOUR SPEECH

After you have decided on the pattern, your next step is to develop or expand the body of the speech. Again, you must consider the purpose of your talk. If your purpose is to inform, you may wish to use certain verbal devices that will clarify, expand upon, or describe your subject. If you wish to modify belief, you may use other verbal aids that prove or reinforce your contentions.

Speech supports

The verbal and audio-visual devices that give meat to the skeleton of a speech are called *speech supports*. You can choose from the following typical speech supports when planning your speech.

Definition. The meaning of a word or concept is its definition. A definition may take the form of a classification, comparison, or example, among others. To define *should,* you might say, "By the word *should,* we mean *ought to;* that a moral obligation exists to adopt the proposal." Operational definitions can also be used to clarify a concept. They describe the process used in order to "get to" the word. For example, a cake consists of one cup of flour, two eggs, and so on. The recipe is the definition.

Description. To explain something by referring to sensory data—its size, weight, color, texture, taste, or smell—is to describe it. You could describe someone you met by saying, "She was a tall girl with auburn hair, green eyes, and freckles on her nose. She was in her teens and wore the typical teenage apparel—blue jeans, shirt, and sandals."

Example. An instance, illustration, or case in point that serves to explain or clarify a concept is an example. Example, real and supposed, is a widely used verbal device that is an excellent support for most speeches. During the course of a speech, a speaker may say something like, "We are dependent on other countries for many consumer products. For example, much of our coffee comes from Brazil."

Comparison. To explain something that is unknown by describing its similarities and differences with something known is to compare the two. Showing the relationship or similarities between two things or concepts is also a comparison. "The wallaby, like the kangaroo, is a marsupial," is a comparison.

Contrast. Contrast is the same as comparison, but is usually used to point out differences instead of similarities: "The camel, unlike the dromedary, has two humps on his back."

Statistics. Factual data in numerical form are statistics. "Since the turn of the century, nearly 800,000 United States citizens have been killed by privately owned guns."

Testimony. Statements, usually quotations, of others on matters of fact or opinion are called testimony. In most cases, the value of testimony depends upon the qualifications of the person being quoted.

Audio-visual aids. Materials that can be seen or heard and supplement the spoken speech are called audio-visual aids. Visual materials such as pictures, charts, models, diagrams, and objects and audio materials such as recordings, live music, and artificially produced sounds may make good audio-visual aids. Audio-visual aids are important supports to many speeches and should be used whenever appropriate.

Verbal devices for reinforcement or emphasis

You may sometimes wish to reinforce or emphasize a particular point or part of your speech. There are several verbal devices that may be used for that purpose.

Restatement. Restatement is repetition of a word, phrase, or sentence. "The answer to your question is no, N O, NO!"

Reiteration. Repetition of the same thought or idea in different words is reiteration. "Always watch out for the other driver. In other words, be a defensive driver."

Summaries. A summary reviews the important points made previously. "Let's summarize what we have shown so far . . ."

Slogans, adages, proverbs. "The life you save may be your own."

Rhetorical attention devices. "Now, hear this!" "This is important." "Think about that for awhile."

DEVELOPING THE INTRODUCTION

Salutation

It is up to the speaker to determine the type of salutation, or phrase of greetings most appropriate to the occasion. The standard "Ladies and Gentlemen," "Friends," or "Fellow Members" may be used, or a verbal salutation may be omitted entirely and the audience acknowledged with a nod of the head and a slight pause. If you are introduced by a chairperson, it is customary to say, for example, "Mr. Chairperson, Friends," or, "Thank you, Mr. Chairperson. Ladies and Gentlemen."

The introduction

The introduction of your speech should achieve three goals. It should: (1) Gain the attention of your audience and indicate the general subject; (2) Motivate the audience to listen to your talk; and (3) Indicate specifically what you plan to do.

Gaining attention

You must assume that the audience is inattentive. It is up to you to gain their immediate and close attention. A few methods of gaining attention follow.

1. *Startling statement.* "Forty thousand people died last year in automobile accidents." (Speech on safe driving.)

2. *Quotation.* " 'The world's biggest heavy industry is war.' Thus says an editorial in the *Dublin Opinion*." (Speech on war)

3. *Anecdote.* "Overheard in a restaurant: 'I wish they'd take these mirrors off the cigarette machines. I hate looking at a weak man.' " (Speech on cigarette smoking.)

4. *Rhetorical question.* Pose a stimulating question to the audience and answer it. "What would you do if you scraped an unoccupied car in a parking lot while you were driving?" (Speech on ethics.)

5. *Reference to the audience or occasion.* Sometimes it may be politic to comment on the audience or occasion. Usually this comment can be followed by your attention-opener.

6. *Audio-visual aid.* Audio-visual aids make excellent attention-getters for many speeches. Use such aids whenever you can.

In all these sample openings, the speakers have indicated, in a general way, the probable topic of their talks. This serves as a guidepost to the audience of what to expect. Avoid the nonsequitur introduction, in which the speech does not follow logically from the introductory remarks.

Motivating the audience to listen

Motivating the audience to listen is probably the most important and most neglected part of the introduction. Too many times, speakers interested in a particular subject assume that the audience shares their interest. Not necessarily so! For example, one student began his speech with, "Today, I'm going to talk about old glass." His audience appeared indifferent. The speaker's next statement was, "Old glass can be studied on the basis of three historical periods." The faces in the audience remained blank. The speaker had failed to kindle interest in his subject. There was no motivation to listen.

Another speaker began his talk, "Do you want to make some extra money this summer, maybe two or three hundred dollars?" The members of the audience sat up straight, eyes wide open. "Just look through your attics and basements for old glass. It's worth a lot of money, and I'm going to tell you how to recognize the valuable pieces." The audience listened attentively to every word of that speech. This is motivation—showing the audience how they can benefit by listening to a particular speech.

Motivate your audience by showing how the speech will help them, why it is to their interest to listen, what they will gain by listening. If a subject seems difficult to motivate, you can always appeal to intellectual curiosity.

Stating the speech purpose

The purpose sentence of a speech indicates what you are attempting to do, what you propose. An audience likes to be forewarned.

Sometimes the purpose sentence can be combined with the attention step or the motivation step. For example, in the "old glass" speech, the sentence, "It's worth a lot of money, and I'm going to tell you how to recognize the valuable pieces," serves as both the motivation step and the purpose sentence. In other speeches, however, it may be necessary to specifically announce your topic or point of view. For example, "This morning I would like to examine with you some safety rules to observe when driving a car."

In some cases, it might be best not to "announce" your topic or point of view. If your subject is highly controversial—Mercy killing, Abortion, Capital punishment, for example—it is generally wise to avoid any direct statement of purpose and to persuade by implication or veiled suggestion without announcing your own convictions.

Borden's formula

Professor Borden, in *Public Speaking As Listeners Like It,* suggests the following formula based on the feelings of an audience during a typical speech.[1] Make sure that your speech takes account of these silent audience reactions.

1. Ho, hum!   When speaker stands up to talk.
2. Why bring that up? When speaker announces topic.
3. For instance?   When speaker makes a statement.
4. So what?   When speaker gives example.

Your introduction should provide for the first two audience reactions and your speech proper should satisfy the last two.

DEVELOPING THE CONCLUSION

The conclusion of your speech is important since the audience is apt to remember your concluding remarks more vividly than the rest of your speech. Avoid such conclusions as, "Well, I guess that's it," or, "I guess that's all I have to say on the subject." These statements cause the audience to feel that you are either poorly prepared or inadequate as a speaker. Nor should you end your speech with "I thank you." If you have done a good job, the audience will thank *you*. Make your conclusion definite. Be sure that the audience understands by your words and voice that the talk is ended.

Three suggestions for concluding your talk are:

1. Summarize the main points of your talk. Itemize the main points, using numerals or letters if there are more than two main ideas.

2. Reiterate the motivation for the talk and repeat the main idea or purpose of your talk. A good closing statement is: "Automobile accidents affect your health, your property, your life. So, when you get behind that wheel after this meeting, drive carefully and watch out for the other fellow."

3. Appeals for action or support are often effective: "All of you know what our needs are so let's get behind the fund-raising committee and make this year's drive the best drive yet!"

WORDING THE SPEECH

Although you are preparing an extemporaneous speech, you will choose words and grammatical structure in your practice sessions. You should, therefore, become familiar with the language style used in speeches. *It is not always the same as that used in written discourse.*

Try to incorporate the following oral language concepts into your practice sessions:

1. Avoid long, involved sentences. Better to use two or three short sentences.

2. Feel free to use sentence fragments or phrases rather than complete sentences if the meaning is clear.

3. Use a direct, intimate style. Take the audience into your confidence. Talk about *our* problem, *your* opportunities, *you* folks at this meeting. Use plenty of personal pronouns. Make your audience feel directly involved.

4. Use words that express exactly what you mean. Use simple everyday words rather than unfamiliar words, but avoid hackneyed words and phrases. "Unaccustomed as I am to public speaking" and "It gives me great pleasure to be speaking here tonight," are glaring examples of worn out expressions.

5. Use concrete, real-life examples rather than abstract, imaginary examples. Better to say, "There was an automobile accident yesterday on Route Ten. Johnny Smith, a four-year old, was injured," than to say "Let's assume that a child was in an automobile accident." The second statement lacks realism and authenticity. It does not provoke attention and interest.

6. Use vivid, colorful language, language that appeals to the senses. Use figurative language—simile, metaphor, and personification. Note the vivid language used by Sir Winston Churchill in his famous "blood, toil, tears, and sweat" speech:

> "You ask, what is our policy? I say it is to wage war by land, sea, and air. War with all our might and with all the strength God has given us, and to wage war against a monstrous tyranny never surpassed in the dark and lamentable catalogue of human crime. That is our policy. You ask, what is our aim? I can answer in one word. It is victory. Victory at all costs—victory in spite of all terrors—victory, however hard and long the road may be, for without victory there is no survival."

> Make sure your speech has a three-point introduction, careful organization, numerous speech supports, verbal reinforcement, and a memorable conclusion.

Projects

1. Indicate which organizational pattern would be most suitable for five different speech topics. For example, "Changing a tire" should be chronological.
2. Apply three or more speech supports, for example, definition, comparison, or statistics, to some of the selected topics.
3. Practice using one or more reinforcement devices for your selected topics.
4. Prepare a one minute introduction to one of your topics. Also, be ready to present your conclusion to the class.

Notes

1. Richard C. Borden, *Public Speaking as Listeners Like It,* (New York: Harper & Brothers, 1935)

Suggested Readings

Capp, Glen R. and G. Richard Capp, Jr., *Basic Oral Communication,* 2nd ed., (Englewood Cliffs, N.J.: Prentice-Hall, Inc., 1976).

Chapter 8, "Selecting and Evaluating Supporting Material," is a helpful chapter on supporting material. The authors explain the forms of support in some detail and list many examples of each form.

Hart, Roderick P., Gustav W. Friedrich, and William D. Brooks, *Public Communication,* (New York: Harper and Row, 1975).

Chapter 6, "The Message as Resource," goes into considerable detail on the message of the speech as it involves personal revelation, factual material, and relevance to the audience. Chapter 7 deals with the barriers to effective communication, a method of applying certain basic themes to any speech subject, and a detailed list of the factors of attention.

SMILE, DON'T FROWN!
YOU'RE IN THE PUBLIC EYE

Photograph by Jerald W. Rogers.

Chapter 14

Delivering Your Speech

Performance Objectives

After studying chapter 14, you should be able to:

1. Describe how a speaker should prepare for giving a speech.
2. Describe how a speaker should behave when approaching and on the speaking platform.
3. Explain the use of audio-visual aids in a speech.
4. Present and discuss five ways to present an impromptu talk.
5. List and explain some do's and don'ts for introducing another speaker.
6. Discuss the recommended procedures for giving four different ceremonial speeches.

BEFORE THE SPEECH OCCASION

A day or two before you give your speech, it is wise to check the physical facilities of the meeting place and the program for the meeting.

1. What is the seating arrangement? Are the chairs adequately placed in reference to the speaker's position?
2. Is a lectern available? Is it adequately lighted? Is there a microphone?
3. Are there facilities for audio-visual aids? A.C. electric outlets? A blackboard? Display stands? A viewing screen?
4. Is a program of events available? Who is the chairperson? Are other speakers on the program? What is the speaking order?

Advance attention to these details can prevent possible embarrassment and ensure a more successful speaking experience.

AT THE SPEECH OCCASION

The following checklist, though detailed, should be studied carefully in order to present an effective talk. Note especially those items that apply to your particular situation.

Before going to the platform. Can you pass public inspection? Is your clothing arranged? Are buttons buttoned, zippers zipped, snaps snapped? Once you approach the speaker's platform, either from the audience or an anteroom, you are *in the public eye.*

Do you have your speaking materials in order? If you plan to use notes they should be on three-by-five inch cards that can be held out of view in the palm of your hand. If you plan to use visual aids they should be arranged in an orderly fashion so that you can present them readily.

Approaching the platform. Walk briskly, and with confidence, to the platform. Try to feel congenial. Smile! Avoid any premature comments or asides. If you are to sit prior to your talk, do so gracefully. Do not cross your legs.

At the lectern. Face front, look at your audience, and wait for attention. Acknowledge the audience with a nod and then begin your introductory remarks. On more formal occasions, it may be appropriate to use a verbal salutation. For example, "Thank you Mr. Chairperson. (Pause) Distinguished guests, Ladies and Gentlemen."

Avoid using a lectern if possible. It only hides you from your audience. If it is necessary to use a lectern, do not overuse it. Move about from one side to the other. If you are using a microphone, however, it will be necessary to stay behind the lectern within microphone range. Do *not rest* on the lectern; do not grip its edges.

Stand with your weight on both feet. Your feet should be about ten inches apart with one foot slightly advanced. Move about the platform, especially when introducing a new part of your speech, but avoid meaningless, nervous movements such as pacing back and forth. Keep your arms at your sides so that you can supplement your words with gestures when appropriate. Do *not* fold your arms across your chest or clasp your hands behind your back. Do *not* put your hands in your pockets. Avoid toying with a pencil, chalk, or any other object.

Look at your audience all of the time. Move your head from side to side so that you appear to be talking to every person before you. Make direct eye to eye contact with your listeners. Do *not* look over the heads or down at the knees of your audience.

Speak in a conversational style. Imagine that you are talking to a small group of friends. Avoid any type of artificiality such as pompous oratory or overly dramatic movements.

In order to make your important ideas stand out, use considerable emphasis and vocal variety. Speak at a slower rate than in conversation. Most beginners speak too rapidly. Don't be afraid to pause. A pause at the right time will tend to center attention on your next thought.

Control your articulation and pronunciation. Remember, this is a formal speech situation. Use your very best speech. When you have finished your talk acknowledge the audience with a nod and return to your seat. Do *not* say "Thank you."

USING AUDIO-VISUAL AIDS

It has been suggested previously that audio-visual aids make valuable supporting devices for many speeches and that such aids should be used when they will contribute to the speaker's purpose. Following are some suggestions on the use of audio-visual aids.

1. Audio-visual aids should not dominate the verbal content of your speech. Use such aids as a supplement to your speech, not as the speech itself.
2. Be sure that the visual aids used are large enough to be seen easily by

all members of the audience. A small photograph, for example, should not be used since it cannot be seen by all of your listeners.

3. Avoid passing out visual material such as a photograph to your listeners during your speech. Such material will distract a part of your audience when they should be attending to your speech.

4. Always practice using the audio-visual aid before you give your speech. For example, if you are going to use a record player, try in advance the volume control, the on-off switch, and general operating instructions. If you plan to play a segment of a recording, mark the starting point with chalk or red tape. If you are going to use a visual aid, know in advance, how you are going to use it. For example, if you plan to show a map, how are you going to hold it up for viewing? Will you use tape, tacks, or a map stand? Is a pointer available?

5. When describing or using a visual aid, be sure that you do not block the view of the audience. Stand to one side of the item displayed and use a pointer, if necessary, to explain it. Be sure to maintain maximum eye contact with your audience. Do not become overly engrossed in the aid itself, but do become engrossed with presenting your ideas to your audience.

IMPROMPTU SPEAKING

There will be many occasions, such as civic meetings, business affairs, and certain social situations, when you will be called upon "to say a few words" without advance notice. The "few words" you say will be an *impromptu talk,* which means it is unprepared and unrehearsed. Of course you *will* be prepared, in part, since you will use material from your general fund of knowledge, your past experiences, and from previous extemporaneous speeches that you have given. But, even with this awareness of the nature of impromptu, you will have little time to search your memory and organize your thoughts.

Here are some guidelines to make your impromptu talks more effective.

1. Determine your point of view or conclusion on the subject at hand before you begin and then work to establish that point of view or conclusion. Generally, you should try to develop one or two points that will support your conclusion. For example, if you were on the social committee of a club and the question was the desirability of having a club picnic, your impromptu talk might discuss the advantages of

such an outing and recommend time and place, leading to your conclusion that you favor a club picnic. Or, if you were a guest at a debate banquet and were asked to speak, you might decide to show the
values of debating. Your speech, then, would give examples of
values and advantages of debating to establish your conclusion.

2. In opening your talk, make any necessary acknowledgements to the
chairperson or audience, comment, if desirable, on the purpose of
the meeting, and then begin developing your theme toward your
planned conclusion.

3. Avoid unnecessary rambling. Get to the point. If good supporting
devices come to mind, use them, but keep the speech short.

4. Avoid "backtracking." This only accentuates your lack of organization and confuses the audience. It is true that most of us think in
retrospect of what we *should* have said, but these afterthoughts have
no place in the speech.

5. When the time comes to state your conclusion, do so with conviction.
Indicate with your voice that you have completed your remarks, that
the speech is ended.

> Impromptu talks should be aimed toward
> a predetermined conclusion. Avoid ram-
> bling. Get to the point. Keep it short.

SPECIAL OCCASION SPEECHES

There are some speeches that are not readily classifiable into the
usual "general purpose" grouping. Such presentations, speeches for
special occasions, include introducing other speakers and speeches of a
ceremonial nature.

Introducing another speaker

You may often be called upon to introduce another speaker. You
should be able to make such an introduction with grace and ease. Keep
in mind the purpose of the introduction. You are acting as an interme-
diary between the speaker and his audience. You are fulfilling the function of the speech introduction; that is, gaining attention, indicating the
topic, and motivating the audience to listen. Be sure to accomplish these

requirements in your presentation. Here are some additional suggestions:

Get basic information in advance. Find out the speaker's name, title, employer, educational background (if pertinent), work experience, honors, and so on. Find out why he or she is qualified to speak on the subject. Get the specific title of the speech and the general content, or outline, of the talk.

Some do's and don'ts in presentation. Be sincere and friendly. Give a brief background on the speaker. Stress the experience and education that qualifies him or her to speak on the subject. Show that the subject is timely, and important to the audience. Give a background of the subject without infringing upon the speaker's material. Be brief! Too many jokes have been told about long, tiresome introductions.

Don't make jokes at the expense of the speaker. Don't flatter the speaker to the point of embarrassment. Don't say too much about the speaker's subject. Let the speaker say it. Don't be pompous, artifical, or long-winded.

Delivering the speech. (Courtesy of Bryn Mawr College.)

Sample introduction of another speaker. "Ladies and Gentlemen: Every single day, in the United States of America, there are fifty deaths caused by guns. Fifty deaths per day; two every hour; over 18,000 every year. Some of these tragedies are accidental, some are suicides, but most of them are murders. Friends! This wholesale slaughter of our people must stop. Something has to be done—and soon.

"We are fortunate to have as our speaker today a man well qualified to speak on the subject of gun control—our police chief, Captain John Davis. Captain Davis has been on the force here for over ten years. A graduate of Temple University, he spent a year at the Police Academy in New York City and five years as a plainclothes investigator in that city. When Captain Davis came here, he supervised and staffed our crime laboratory and then moved up to the job of chief. Here is a man who knows his job and knows a great deal about guns. The subject of today's talk is gun control legislation. Ladies and Gentlemen, Captain John Davis."

CEREMONIAL SPEECHES

Speech of presentation

The purpose of a speech of presentation is to present an award to an individual or group for some special accomplishment or distinction. The presentation should be sincere, friendly, and brief.

If you are presenting the award, you will be at the lectern and the recipient should be seated, or standing, on your right for ease in presenting the trophy, plaque, or other award object.

To begin the presentation speech, face the audience and give the background information on the award. Mention the group presenting it, the reason for the presentation, and give information on the recipient. Refer to the recipient, when appropriate, with a gesture or nod in his direction. When the time comes to make the actual presentation, turn, face the recipient, and address him by name. On this cue, the recipient will stand and move toward the center of the platform. You will now end the verbal presentation, usually by repeating the basic information concerning the award and the recipient. Then, holding the award in your right hand, present it to the left hand of the recipient. You may proffer your hand for a handshake. Once you have seated yourself the recipient will give his acceptance speech.

Acceptance speech

The purpose of the acceptance speech is to acknowledge an award or honor. The speaker should be modest, sincere, and brief.

If you are accepting an award, keep your remarks low-key. Express your thanks for the award and your gratitude for the opportunity to participate in the group. Cite your fellow members, family, or friends who served as good examples or who aided you in any way. Remember that this is a courtesy speech; share the glory and keep the speech short.

The speech of welcome

A speech of welcome is similar to introducing a speaker, except that the emphasis will be on the person being welcomed rather than a speech topic.

If you are the welcoming speaker, it is important to find out all you can about the person being welcomed; hometown, vocation, education, accomplishments, and some information about his family life.

As for the speech itself, the keynote should be friendly sincerity.

You are saying, in effect, "We are your friends. We want you to like us. We like and respect you and hope that the feeling is mutual." Much of this warmth and sincerity is conveyed in the *manner of speaking*, including facial expression and gesture.

The content of the speech might include some information about the welcoming group, information on and praise of the visitor, and a few remarks about the future of the guest.

Responding to a welcome

Modesty is the essence of a speech responding to welcome. Express thanks and appreciation to the chairperson for the kind words and to the group as participants in the welcome. Minimize your own accomplishments, especially if the welcoming speaker has been overly ardent, and focus attention, instead, on your great interest in the group and your pleasure in being with the group. Be warm, be sincere, be brief.

Projects

1. Speech introduction
   a. Select a subject for an imaginary speech. (See suggested topics in chapter 12)
   b. Prepare a three-point introduction that gains attention and indicates the topic, motivates the audience to listen, and gives a purpose sentence.
   c. Practice the introduction. Do not use notes. The introduction should not take over two minutes.
   d. Tape the introduction using the techniques of good speech delivery.
   e. Evaluate the tape as Fair, Good, or Excellent. If you grade yourself Fair, repeat the project.

2. Prepare a three-minute speech to inform in which you use a visual aid.
   a. Divide the subject, if possible, into its logical parts. Determine what method of organization should be used. Outline the body of your speech.
   b. Prepare an introduction and conclusion, and enter them in your outline.
   c. Look up any additional information you need for your talk and add this to your outline.
   d. Use your outline to practice your talk, including the presentation of your visual aid. Have a friend or member of your family listen. Ask for comments and criticism.
   e. Tape your talk exactly as you would give it in an audience situation. Check your taped speech for time, fluency, vocal variety, and emphasis. Be your own critic. Repeat the project if you feel the speech was unsatisfactory.

3. Impromptu talk
   a. Select one of the subjects suggested in chapter 12.
   b. Tape a one- to two-minute impromptu talk on this subject following the instructions given previously, or as follows:
      (1) Determine your point of view or conclusion on the selected subject.
      (2) Introduce the subject in one or two sentences.

(3) Give one or more supporting statements to reinforce your conclusion.

(4) State your conclusion.

4. Prepare a five-minute speech to inform on any subject you choose. Prepare an outline as suggested in project 2. Include the following supporting devices in the body of your outline:

a. Two or more examples.

b. Two or more quotations.

c. One comparison and one contrast.

d. Some statistical data.

Practice the speech as suggested in project 2. Tape it and evaluate your performance. Repeat the project if the speech is unsatisfactory.

5. Volunteer for a short reading or speaking assignment in your church, club, or civic group. Practice and tape your talk before giving it. Report the results of this assignment to your instructor.

6. Impromptu speaking exercise. The first speaker begins by giving a two-minute talk on either of the choices for #1. The second speaker speaks on #2, and so on.

1. a. What should be done to reduce unemployment?

b. What can be done to ensure an adequate supply of energy?

2. a. What policy should the United States adopt toward China?

b. What policy should the United States adopt toward arm shipments to foreign countries?

3. a. What changes, if any, should be made in our divorce laws?

b. What should our attitude be toward abortion?

4. a. What should our attitude be toward capital punishment?

b. How, if at all, should teachers punish misbehaving school children?

5. a. Who should go to college?

b. What is wrong, if anything, with health care in the United States?

6. a. What attitude should we have toward a state lottery system?

b. What policy should our county adopt toward population growth?

7. a. Is woman's place in the home?

b. What is your favorite gripe?

8. a. What should our attitude be toward state income taxes?

   b. What can be done to lessen air pollution in this area?

9. a. What policy should the federal government adopt on the sale and use of marijuana?

   b. What policy should your state adopt regarding prostitution?

10. a. What attitude should we have toward bussing children for integration?

    b. What role should women play in the armed services?

11. a. Are women really the weaker sex?

    b. What policy should your state adopt toward pornography?

12. a. What attitude should we have toward trial marriage?

    b. What attitude should we have toward homosexuals?

13. a. What is wrong, if anything, with television?

    b. Should topless waitresses be banned?

14. a. What can be done to combat inflation?

    b. Should off-track betting be legal?

15. a. What attitude should we have toward euthenasia (mercy killing)?

    b. How could your college be improved?

16. a. Should suicide be legalized?

    b. What legislation, if any, should be adopted on gun control?

17. a. What legislative program, if any, should be adopted to control population growth in the United States?

    b. What new policy, if any, should be adopted regarding the food-stamp program?

18. a. Does the federal Government have too much power?

    b. Should the United States adopt a system of socialized medicine?

19. a. Is a college education beneficial?

    b. My idea of a good party.

20. a. How to get ahead in life.

    b. How to be happy.

Suggested Readings

Bryant, Donald C. and Karl R. Wallace, *Oral Communication: A Short Course in Speaking*, 4th ed. (Englewood Cliffs, N.J.: Prentice-Hall, Inc., 1976) See Chap. 6, "Visual and Audio Materials," Chap. 10, "Principles of Delivery," and Chap. 11, "Special Forms: Occasional Speeches, The Public Interview."

Oliver, Robert T., *Making Your Meaning Effective*, (Boston: Holbrook Press, Inc., 1971) See Chap. 6, "Presenting Your Speech," Chap. 7, "Making Your Style Reflect Yourself," and Chap. 8, "Building A Vocabulary for Your Needs."

TO STRENGTHEN BELIEF

OR TO CHANGE BELIEF?

Photograph by Jerald W. Rogers.

Chapter 15

Persuasive Speaking

Performance Objectives

After studying chapter 15, you should be able to:

1. Explain the nature of the speech to strengthen belief and give examples of situations they are typically used in.
2. List the five general types of motive appeals and give several specific examples of each.
3. Explain the nature of the speech to change belief, and give examples of situations they are typically used in.
4. List the guidelines for choosing a subject for a speech to change belief.
5. Explain the difference between questions of fact, value, and policy.
6. Explain the four steps in a problem-solution development of a policy-type speech to change belief.
7. Explain how to research materials for a speech to change belief.
8. Define evidence and give the general tests of evidence and the test of the source of evidence.
9. Distinguish between evidence and reasoning and describe inductive and deductive reasoning.
10. List four special techniques in persuasive speaking.

When we grouped speeches according to their general purpose, we found that there were two categories—to strengthen belief and to change belief—that might be considered persuasive-type speeches. Although the techniques of public speaking apply to all types of speeches, there are some elements in preparing and presenting a persuasive speech that deserve special consideration.

THE SPEECH TO STRENGTHEN BELIEF

When your audience is in general agreement with your proposition or speech subject, your speech purpose will probably be to strengthen belief, reinforce attitudes, or urge action. For example, when a minister preaches a sermon, he may ask for deeper convictions of religious belief or urge a greater adherence to moral values. The football coach, addressing the local Boosters Club, may call for more enthusiasm in support of the local team. Or the Republican candidate may urge all the members of his *Republican* audience to go to the polls and vote. In all three cases, the audiences already agree in principle with the speakers but are urged to feel more deeply about their convictions or to take definite action in sup-

port of their beliefs. All three situations, moreover, lend themselves to persuasion through appeals to the needs and wants of the listeners. We are all familiar with magazine and television advertising techniques: the pretty girl in the automobile advertisement, the luscious-looking steak in the food advertisement, or the pathetic orphan in a charity advertisement. These appeals to sex, appetite, and pity are also used in persuasive speaking. Following is a typical list of appeals commonly used in speeches to strengthen belief.

Motive appeals

Basic needs. Nourishment; shelter; protection from injury; avoidance of disease and pain; self preservation.

Wants. Love; sex; companionship; offspring; adventure; security; self-respect; respect of others; group identification; group preservation; material possessions; power over others; freedom from restraint; physical activity; relaxation; excitement; tranquility; reverence; learning; creative work.

Emotions. Love; hate; anger; fear; pity; sympathy; pride; humor.

Values. Patriotism; duty; responsibility; courage; honesty; loyalty; justice; freedom; compassion; modesty; cleanliness.

Sensuousness. A hot sizzling steak; The smell of orange blossoms.

The motives for human belief, attitudes, and action are complex and it is quite reasonable to believe that any change is motivated by several factors. The persuasive speaker, therefore, will use those appeals that are the most appropriate to bring about the desired audience response.

Examples of motive appeal

"The life you save may be your own."   (Self-preservation)
"My country, right or wrong."   (Patriotism)
"No man is an island."   (Group identification)

"Give me liberty or give me death."   (Freedom)
"Everyone of voting age should vote."   (Duty)
"A hot, sizzling steak."   (Sensory pleasures)
"Would you inform on a friend?"   (Loyalty)
"Imagine, a trip down the Colorado river."   (Adventure)

"Everyone deserves an equal opportunity." (Justice)
"These children never had a decent meal." (Pity, group pre-
serivation)

Usually, each motive appeal would be extended and elaborated.
Often, motive appeals can be included in an example or a short narra-
tive. See if you can pick out and label the motive appeals in the following excerpt. Are there any "new" appeals?

"Duty," "honor," "country"—these three hallowed words
reverently dictate what you want to be, what you can be, what you
will be . . . They teach you to be proud and unbending in honest
failure, but humble and gentle in success; not to substitute words
for action; not to seek the path of comfort, but to face the stress and
spur of difficulty and challenge; to learn to stand up to the storm,
but to have compassion on those that fail; to master yourself before
you seek to master others; to have a heart that is clean, a goal that is
high; to learn to laugh, yet never take yourself too seriously; to be
modest so that you will remember the simplicity of true greatness;
the open mind of true wisdom, the meekness of true strength.
—Gen. Douglas McArthur, "Duty, Honor, and Country"

> Use motive appeals to strengthen belief.

THE SPEECH TO CHANGE BELIEF

Speeches to change belief, convince, or urge action, are always
based on a problem or felt need. The speaker in effect is saying that
something is wrong, harmful, unfair, or undesirable; or, Adopt my proposal because it would be beneficial, exciting, fun, or satisfying. On the
other hand, a speaker may defend the status quo, deny the existence of
a problem, or attempt to prove that a proposed change is inadvisable.
The factor that differentiates this particular type of speech from others is
disbelief or disagreement within a certain audience. In other words,
when the speech subject is controversial or the speaker's point of view is
unacceptable to some or all of the audience members, the general purpose of the speech will probably be to *change belief*. If the speaker feels
that some of the listeners are hostile, some indifferent, and some

friendly toward the proposition, he will aim his speech at those listeners who are hostile or indifferent and, at the same time, hope to strengthen the belief of those who favor the proposition.

Selecting a problem or need for a subject

How do we find a suitable problem to use as the subject of a speech? Problems are all around us. We have many more problems than we have solutions. But which of the many problems—local, national, or international—would be most suitable for our purposes? The following guidelines may prove helpful in selecting a subject.

1. Select a problem that is of interest to you and about which you have, or can obtain, information.
2. Select a problem that pertains to your audience.
3. Select a problem that is important and relevant today.
4. Select a problem that can be narrowed to meet the time limit.

Sometimes problems are so big that they force themselves upon us, as do wars, hurricanes, and earthquakes. Or we may inherit certain problems that have always troubled mankind, such as poverty, crime, and disease. A few controversial topics that have been of concern to us recently: birth control, school integration, civil rights, air and water pollution, drug addiction, crime, divorce, abortion, sex education, alcoholism, and welfare. Note that many of these topics deal with national affairs. You may, however, select a local problem or even a problem that concerns only your immediate audience.

Determine the proposition

The proposition states the subject so that it expresses the speaker's point of view. It may be worded in the affirmative or negative. For example:

1. We should (should not) legalize gambling.
2. All divorce laws should (should not) be the same nation-wide.
3. A traffic light should (should not) be installed at the intersection of Main and Elm.
4. Our club should (should not) increase its dues.

The proposition, either stated or implied, is the recommendation or solution that you must prove to the satisfaction of your listeners. In formal debate, the proposition is the title or subject for debate: for example, "Resolved, that all American citizens be guaranteed an annual income."

In most persuasive speeches, the audience will be aware of the proposition and the speaker's point of view on the question. However, if the subject is extremely controversial, for example, open housing legislation, and you have an exceptionally hostile audience, it may be advisable to avoid announcing the proposition or your position on the question and persuade, instead, by presenting your case in the form of veiled suggestion and letting your listeners arrive at their own conclusions.

Analysis of the question

Before developing the body of your speech, you should carefully analyze the problem.

1. Determine the general area of the problem. Is it international, national, or local? Economic, political, or social? How is your audience related to the problem? What can they do to bring about a solution?

2. What general type of problem is involved? Fact? Value? Policy?

   a. *Proposition of fact.* A statement regarding the truth or falsity of an alleged fact is a proposition of fact. "Was the assassination of President Kennedy a political plot?" is such a proposition. Not all questions of fact lend themselves to argumentation. In many instances, facts can be proved in other ways. We do not "argue" the height of a tree; we measure it.

   b. *Proposition of value.* A statement concerning a value judgment is a proposition of value. "School A is superior to School B;" and "Lincoln was our greatest president" are propositions of value. The objections to using such questions for serious persuasive talks are obvious. The questions are ambiguous. What is meant by "superior?" What is meant by "greatest?" And yet, there may be times when it is necessary or desirable to speak on a question of value. If so, standards must be established by which to judge the proposition and/or the "value" words must be carefully defined.

   c. *Proposition of policy.* A statement regarding some future action, implying dissatisfaction with the status quo is a proposition of policy. For example, "China should be admitted to the United Nations." "Property taxes should be lowered." "Our club should sponsor a dance next month." In a proposition of policy, there is a problem or felt need and the proposition is worded as a solution that, it is assumed, will solve the problem or satisfy the felt need. Also, of course, a speaker may defend the status quo and "persuade" against a proposed action.

3. What is the specific nature of the problem? What are the immediate symptoms? Whom does it effect? What are its causes? What attempts have been made to solve it? How does it relate to the present audience?

4. Be able to define all key terms—those in the proposition itself and those related to the problem.

Developing the speech

The speech to change belief usually follows a problem-solution order of development. The following order of steps can be used in planning your speech.

1. Show that there is a problem, that there is a need for change. Prove the extent of the problem; show its effect on your listeners.

2. Show that your solution will eliminate or alleviate the problem.

3. Show that your solution is practical.
   a. that it can be financed
   b. that it can be enforced
   c. that its advantages outweigh its disadvantages
   d. that it will not introduce other problems

4. Show that your solution is the best solution.
   a. that other solutions will not eliminate the problem
   b. that other solutions have serious disadvantages

These four steps become the major divisions of your speech and should be developed as necessary to achieve your purpose. In some cases, you may wish to confine your speech to the presentation of the problem itself, leaving the solution up to the audience, or for later consideration. You will determine the degree of development by the nature of the subject and by your specific purpose in speaking.

Following is a sample outline depicting the four steps of development.

Proposition: The federal government should require the registration of all firearms.

II. Body
  A. The lack of adequate federal gun regulation poses a serious threat to citizens.
    1. Anyone can purchase a gun through a mail-order house.
    2. There were 20,000 fatalities in 1977 due to gunshot wounds. (*Time,* June 21, 1978)
    3. If guns are easily available, the death toll will continue.
  B. Registration of guns will prevent known criminals and minors from obtaining weapons.
  C. Registration is a practical method of control.
    1. Gun retailers will be required to register the purchasers.
    2. Retailers will report purchases to local law-enforcement agencies.
    3. A seven-day waiting period will be required after purchase before delivery is made.
    4. This requirement will not prevent the legitimate individual from purchasing a gun.
  D. Other solutions are unsatisfactory.
    1. Local and state control is unsatisfactory since guns may be purchased through mail-order houses.
    2. Education on use of firearms is inadequate and would not prevent misuse by criminal elements.

Researching the question

1. Read from the general to the specific on the speech topic. First get an overall view of the question and then follow with specific readings based on your four-point outline.
2. Take detailed notes on four-by-six inch cards on everything you read.
3. Keep an open mind as you do your research. Try not to come to a

final point of view until all of the available facts have been investigated.

4. Complete your working outline with the data you have gathered.

Content of the speech to change belief

The speech to change belief is basically a form of argumentation that consists of evidence and reasoning that tend to prove your proposition. Although motive appeals have a definite place in argumentation, an intelligent audience will demand substantial proof before accepting a new point of view. And proof consists of evidence and reasoning.

1. *Evidence.* Evidence consists of facts (events, objects, conditions, relationships) and opinions (judgments based on an observation of the available facts). Evidence may be in the form of examples, case studies, statistics, or testimony. Apply the following tests to the evidence you secure to evaluate its worth.
   a. Does the evidence seem probable? Does it correlate with your past experience and common sense?
   b. Was the observer-reporter physically, mentally, and morally qualified to make and report the observation?
      (1) Was he a trained, objective, impartial observer?
      (2) Was he a trained, objective, impartial reporter?
      (3) In the case of opinion evidence, was the reporter, or original source, an expert by education and experience?
   c. Was the fact observed by others? Do the observations agree?
   d. Is the fact still observable? Can you confirm it personally?
   e. Is the evidence relevant to your proposition? Is it up-to-date?
   f. Is there enough evidence to prove your point?
2. *Reasoning.* Reasoning is the process of arriving at a conclusion when the data pertaining to that conclusion is incomplete. The two most common methods of reasoning are:
   a. Inductive. Reasoning from individual cases to a generalization. This is the poll method. Samples are taken and a conclusion or estimate is made on the basis of the samples. The actual validity of the conclusion is dependent upon the number of samples taken and the representational adequacy of the samples.

b. Deductive. Reasoning from a general premise to a particular conclusion. For example, "Since there are no regulations concerning
the purchase of guns from a mail-order house, a criminal can
easily purchase a gun." Deductive reasoning can be formally
expressed as a syllogism such as:

All persons can purchase guns without restriction.

A criminal is a person.

Therefore, a criminal can purchase a gun without restriction.

Some textbooks in argumentation recognize two other methods of
reasoning—reasoning from analogy (if two things are alike in some
known respects, they are apt to be alike in other unknown respects) and
causal reasoning (this factory has unsatisfactory working conditions,
and, therefore, it can expect a strike). Often, however, these methods of
reasoning are extensions of inductive or deductive reasoning.

Special techniques in persuasion

In general, all of the elements of good delivery apply to the speech
to change belief, but a few additional suggestions may be in order.

1. Use the "yes technique." Begin with points with which your
   audience will agree. Then gradually work into the controversial
   points.
2. Think of probable objections in advance and answer them in your
   speech.
3. It may be desirable to take an apparently neutral stand on a question,
   state the facts as you see them, and let the audience arrive at their
   own conclusions.
4. It is a good technique to cite the objections to your solution but show
   that the advantages of your proposal outweigh the disadvantages.

Use evidence and reasoning to change belief.

Projects

1. The class will discuss their classmates' speeches, giving special attention to these questions:
   a. What is the general purpose of the speech?
   b. What is the specific purpose of the speech?
   c. How did each speaker gain attention, motivate the audience to listen and handle the purpose sentence?
   d. What motive appeals were used?
   e. To what extent, if any, was logical proof used?
   f. How effective was the conclusion?
2. Select a subject for a five-minute speech to strengthen belief.
   a. List your specific purpose for this speech.
   b. List some of the motive appeals that could be used.
   c. Outline your introduction.
3. Present a five-minute speech to strengthen belief to the class.
4. Select a subject for a five-minute speech to change belief.
   a. List your specific purpose for this speech.
   b. List the specific logical arguments that you would use in this speech.
   c. Outline your introduction for this speech.
5. Present a five-minute speech to change belief to the class.
6. Discuss the following speeches.
7. Study and analyze President Carter's address to the United Nations. (See Appendix)

CHILD ABUSE

by Liz Ecker

We all deal with children from one aspect or another—as parents, siblings, baby-sitters, or neighbors. But there are some people who cannot deal with children, and these people have created a problem so great that it has reached epidemic proportions, and that problem is child abuse.

Before we learn what can be done, and what is being done to resolve this situation, we should have an understanding of what child abuse entails.

Who is most likely to be a child abuser? Surprisingly enough, it is the person who had been abused himself as a child. Rather than being sympathetic toward his own child, he takes on a "might makes right" type of attitude and thinks that abusing a child or beating a child can't be so bad, because he turned out to be a good enough person himself, so it must be an alright type of discipline. In a recent survey conducted by three sociologists, it was determined that apart from situations of war or riot, the home has the most violent atmosphere. Twenty percent of the people surveyed hit children with an object, 4.2 percent admitted to "beating up" a kid, 2.8 percent threatened with a knife or gun, and 2.9 percent actually used a gun or a knife on a child. The rather frightening thing about this, besides the actual violence, was that these people felt that theirs was a reasonably acceptable behavior pattern. I'm not going to go into the details of actual physical attrocities that occur, you can read that in newspapers. These stories occur on local, state and national levels.

Another relatively new aspect of child abuse, and indeed, it must be considered as abuse, is children and pornography. I'm not speaking of allowing minors to sneak into X-rated movies or to buy "dirty" magazines, but I'm talking of children being used as subjects of these movies and magazines. There is actually a demand for pornography involving children as young as three years of age. This demand amounts to an annual traffic amounting to one billion dollars. It also seems that it's relatively easy to obtain little "actors and actresses" for these movies. Parents literally sell their children into the movie business; run-aways need quick money, older kids need money to support drug habits, and juveniles working as prostitutes need extra money. It should also be noted that it is estimated that there are 600,000 male and female prostitutes under the age of sixteen in this country.

Finally, there is psychological abuse, and the best term to describe this would be emotional deprivation, and that's self-explanatory.

What can be done? What is being done? In California there is a twenty-four hour hotline service called Parental Stress Service and this operates like any other crisis intervention service. There is also Parents Anonymous, patterned after Alcoholics Anonymous. They have a toll-free number and can be reached by anyone in the country.

Finally, get involved! If you suspect someone of child abuse, try to talk to them; tell them about Parent's Anonymous. If this doesn't work, get help for the child. In Florida, there is a Child Abuse Registry in Jacksonville. You can call them any time, toll free.

It's taken time, but we have made progress with Equal Rights, Women's Rights, and I think we're long overdue for Children's Rights. Will you help with this atrocious problem?[1]

GIVE UP SMOKING

by Cathy Horkavy

If you had read in the newspaper this morning that eating parsley was suspected as a possible cause of three devastating diseases such as lung cancer, bronchitis, and emphysema, it is very easy to guess what would happen. First, you would immediately stop eating parsley, and soon the shipment and sale of parsley would be prohibited by law.

How does cigarette smoking differ? Some of you may say to yourselves, "I don't smoke, how does this concern me?" It concerns all of us, smokers and nonsmokers. In the United States three deadly diseases are on the increase. Chronic bronchitis and emphysema have risen 1,200 percent in the last sixty years, and today, lung cancer claims 54,000 lives a year. One of those lives may be yours or someone very dear to you.

Do all of you know what these noxious fumes do to your body and your delicate breathing mechanism? Let's take a look at some things called cilia. These are little hairlike structures that line your lungs. They are covered with a thin layer of mucus that picks up dirt and debris. These small cilia move back and forth continuously and move this dirt-laden mucus from your lungs to your throat, where you can get rid of the dirt. Smoking one cigarette paralyzes these cilia for a period of twenty minutes.

The next important structures are the mucus cells. These cells produce the mucus that lines the lungs. Ingredients in cigarette smoke can make these mucus cells increase in size and produce too much mucus, which again hinders the action of the cilia.

Third, and most important of all, are the alveoli. These are small, grape-like sacs where air exchange takes place. Cigarette smoking can cause the walls of these sacs to thicken and sometimes rupture. It all adds up to less air for you.

Besides knowing what cigarette smoke can do to your body, can you name the leading ingredients in cigarettes? The first is nitrogen dioxide. This chemical helps promote lung infection. If you were standing on a busy street corner in a highly polluted city, the highest level of nitrogen dioxide in the air would be about three parts per million. By smoking one cigarette, you increase the level of nitrogen dioxide in the air around you to 250 parts per million.

If you stood in a fume-laden garage, the highest level of carbon monoxide that you would breathe would be about 300 parts per million. By smoking one cigarette, you raise the level in the air around you to 42, 000 parts per million.

The tar of cigarettes, that brown sticky stuff that gets all over your fingers, contains ten known cancer-causing chemicals.

Nicotine, the poison we worry about, is marketed as a powerful insecticide called "Black Leaf 40."

Cigarettes not only contain harmful chemicals, they also contain harmful metals. Cadmium is found in cigarettes and causes kidney damage, lung damage, and cancer of the testicles. Lead causes severe nervous system damage, and fluoride causes migraines, muscle weakness, and arthritis.

If facts and figures don't interest you, think of things another way. Imagine Jane, a beautiful college co-ed, going up to Joe, the star football player. It's not only the smoke smell that clings to her clothes that keeps him from asking her for a date, but after a whiff of her breath, he finishes their conversation completely.

For those of you who watch your pennies, by smoking one pack of cigarettes a day you are spending, on an average, $225 a year just to smoke.

If you eat a balanced diet, get enough exercise and rest, you can expect your health to benefit. The same is true if you refrain from smoking, but another important advantage is obtained. By not smoking you encourage others not to smoke. In addition, you are setting a good example for your neighbors, your spouse, and your children to follow. By not smoking, you make smoking less socially acceptable.

Even if you don't quit, you can help public health. Discuss your feelings openly, admit that it's just too hard to quit, and discourage others from smoking.

And for those of you who have never smoked, keep up the good work.

Remember, an outstanding man in the American medical field, the Surgeon General, "has determined that cigarette smoking is dangerous to your health."[2]

Notes

1. Liz Ecker, *Child Abuse,* an unpublished speech delivered in a class at Manatee Junior College on April 6, 1977.
2. Cathy Horkavy, *Give Up Smoking!,* an unpublished speech delivered in a class at Manatee Junior College on April 6, 1977.

Suggested Readings

Freeley, Austin J., *Argumentation and Debate: Rational Decision Making,* 4th ed. (Belmont, Cal.: Wadsworth Publishing Co., 1976).

This is a comprehensive textbook on debating. It covers the debate process from the selection of the debate topic through the preparation and presentation of the debate speech. The book contains a detailed analysis of evidence, reasoning, and fallacies.

Kahane, Howard, *Logic and Contemporary Rhetoric—The Use of Reason In Everyday Life,* 2nd ed. (Belmont, Cal.: Wadsworth Publishing Co., 1976).

This book is a practical supplement to a study of persuasion. It contains many examples of fallacious reasoning in current political and advertising claims. Also included are many exercises in detecting fallacies of reasoning.

Minnick, Wayne C., *The Art of Persuasion,* 2nd ed. (New York: Houghton Mifflin Co., 1968).

This is a well-organized textbook on persuasion. It includes both the logical and psychological aspects of persuasion with a final chapter on the ethics of persuasion. The book has excellent documentation.

Simons, Herbert W., *Persuasion: Understanding, Practice, and Analysis* (Reading, Mass.: Addison-Wesley Publishing Co., 1976).

This contemporary book on persuasion is designed to help the reader understand persuasion, practice persuasion effectively, and analyze the persuasion of others. The book contains many diagrams, charts, and references that help clarify the technical concepts of persuasion.

Appendix: Student Projects

PERSONAL INVENTORY

Name_____ Age _____

Local _____ Phone_____
   Address

_____
                          ZIP

Your immediate family (for example, father, mother, one sister): _____

_____

Do you live with your family?_____

Schools attended	Town and State	Dates
Elementary		
High		
Other		

Your educational and vocational plans_____

_____

Magazines that you read regularly _____

_____

Hobbies, sports, pastimes_____

_____

Television programs that you enjoy_____

_____

Cities, states, and countries you have visited_____

_____

Do you work?_____ If so, where?_____Hours a week_____

Rate yourself on the following:

	Poor	Fair	Good
Pronunciation			
Vocabulary			
Fluency			
Adequate loudness			
Vocal variety			
Conversational ability			
Social poise			
Group discussion			
Public Speaking			

SELF-EVALUATION INVENTORY ON SPEECH: COMMUNICATION EXTRAS

Directions: Score yourself on each of the following questions as follows:
1 = Poor, 2 = Fair, 3 = Average, 4 = Good, and, 5 = Excellent.

Speech traits

1. I am usually neat in my person and attire. _____

2. I enjoy meeting and talking to new acquaintances. _____

3. I maintain a good posture whether standing or sitting. _____

4. When speaking, I look my listener in the eye. _____

5. I speak without nervous movements or facial grimaces. _____

6. I supplement my vocal speech with adequate gestures. _____

7. I supplement my vocal speech with facial expressiveness. _____

8. My speech is generally free from "er-uh" hesitations. _____

9. When speaking, I use an adequate loudness level. _____

10. When I speak, I usually am clearly understood. _____

Total _____

Listening traits

1. In a conversation, I listen more than I speak. _____

2. I pay attention, even when the speaker is boring. _____

3. When listening, I do not interrupt the speaker. _____

4. When listening, I look at the speaker. _____

5. When listening, I encourage the speaker with facial expressions. _____

6. I listen even if I disagree with the speaker.   _____

7. I generally remember what is being said.   _____

8. I take notes in a lecture course.   _____

9. I refrain from finishing a speaker's thought.   _____

10. Generally, I am a sympathetic listener.   _____

Total _____

_____

Grand Total _____

Ice-Breaker Projects

The following activities are get-acquainted exercises. The projects should be conducted during the first week of class meetings.

The class constitutes the membership of The College Speech Club. Elections of officers is on the agenda of the day. The members of the club (all students in the class) prepare a one-page ballot with a column of numbers—1, 2, 3, and so on—one for each member of the club. After the ballots have been prepared, members of the class take turns coming forward, writing their numbers and names on the blackboard, acknowledging the class with a nod, and returning to their seats. Each class member, presumably electing the club president, votes by assigning each candidate a score from 1-100. Candidate #1 automatically receives a score of 50 percent and each following candidate is given a score higher or lower than 50 percent, depending upon his or her qualifications for the presidency. There should be no ties. When all of the students have presented themselves, each voter tallies his or her ballot by assigning a 3 to the highest-scoring candidate, a 2 to the second highest, and a 1 to the third highest. The ballots are collected by two appointed "volunteers" who tabulate the vote. The three "candidates" receiving the highest total scores will be announced by the instructor as the president, vice president, and secretary-treasurer, respectively, of The College Speech Club. The new officers will come to the front and sit facing the class.

Discussion questions

a. What qualities should a candidate have to be an officer of the club?
b. What was the basis for your vote?
c. Did sex play a role in your selections?
d. Did you know any of the candidates before you voted? Did this factor influence your vote?
e. Did the name of a candidate influence your vote?
f. Did handwriting influence your vote?
g. How important is appearance in making personality judgments?
h. What was the purpose of this experiment?

The members of the class form dyads (pairs) and the members of each dyad interview each other for ten minutes. Then, the class sits in a circle and each member introduces his or her partner and tells three items of interest about him or her, for example, vocational plans, hobbies, and travels. (It is suggested that one member of each dyad introduces his or her partner during the first round, and that the other member introduces his or her partner in the second round.)

The members of the class sit in a circle. One member introduces him- or herself. The next person in the circle repeats the name and gives his or her own name. The third person will repeat both of the previous names and give his or her name, and so on. See how many names can be remembered before beginning again.

The class members are seated in a circle. Each member prepares a name tent (a 4" x 6" card folded in the middle to form a tent) with his or her full name printed in bold letters on both slopes of the tent. Each student supplys the following information on a separate piece of paper:

Name	_____
Sex	_____
Age	_____
Height	_____
Hometown	_____
High school	_____
Major	_____
Hobbies	_____

After the information sheets are completed, they are redistributed throughout the class so that each student has some one else's information sheet. Each student, in turn, then reads aloud the information sheet in his or her possession, *omitting the name of the person it is from.* The class members then guess the name of the person described on the information sheet. *Note:* The tent names should be saved and used for all future group activities.

QUESTIONS FOR PERSONALITY INTERVIEW

Cooperative	Do you like to study with a friend? Explain.
	Do you believe in teamwork? Explain.
Courteous	Do you apologize when you have committed a social blunder?
	Would you give up your seat on a bus for an older person?
Dependable	Are you usually prompt and dependable? Elaborate.
	How many absences did you have last term? Explain.
Generous	Have you ever contributed to a charitable organization?
	Would you lend your car to a friend for a weekend? Explain.
Just	If you scraped the fender of a parked car, would you leave a note?
	If an eccentric old lady offered you $5000 for your battered old Volkswagon, would you sell?
Kind	What is your attitude toward animal pets? Elaborate.
	Describe the last time you helped some one as a favor.
Peaceable	If someone rudely pushed you in a line, what would you do?
	When did you last resort to physical violence? Explain.
Sociable	When you are with a group of people, do you enjoy yourself?
	What is your idea of a good party? Give details.
Creative	Have you ever written a story, poem, or created an art form?
	Have you ever invented anything? Explain.
Determined	Do you usually finish everything you start? Give examples.
	How do you rate yourself in perseverence? Give an example.
Dynamic	Are you a lively, active person? Explain. (Interviewer should also judge this trait by observation.)
Efficient	You must be in New York City tomorrow noon for a three-day convention. Describe your preparations in detail.
Informed	Name the president and the vice president of the United States.
	Tell something about their politics, their families, and so on.

Optimistic   Are you a cheerful person? Are you generally happy? Explain.

Is your glass of Coke half full or half empty? Explain.

Self-reliant   Could you make it through school on your own? Explain.

If you had the materials and tools, could you build a house?

LOGIC PROBLEMS

1. A man has a fox, a goose, and a bucket of grain. He wants to row them across the river in a boat but can take only one at a time. Since the fox will eat the goose and the goose will eat the grain if let alone, how does the man get the three across the river?

2. A man and his wife each weigh one hundred pounds. Their two sons each weigh fifty pounds. How does the man get his family across the river in a rowboat if the rowboat holds only one hundred pounds?

3. A person looking at a portrait said, "Brothers and sisters, I have none. But that man's father is my father's son." What relation was the speaker to the subject of the portrait?

4. A ship is at anchor. Over its side hangs a rope ladder with rungs a foot apart. the tide rises at the rate of eight inches per hour. At the end of six hours, how much of the ladder will remain above water, assuming that eight feet were above water when the tide began to rise?

5. There are two jars of equal capacity. In the first jar there is one amoeba. In the second jar there are two amoebas. An amoeba can reproduce itself in three minutes. It takes the two amoebas in the second jar three hours to fill the jar to capacity. How long does it take the one amoeba in the first jar to fill that jar to capacity?

6. A visitor to the zoo asked how many birds and beasts were in the zoo. The zoo keeper replied that there were thirty heads and one hundred feet. How many birds and how many beasts were in the zoo?

7. If one hundred books are placed on a bookshelf in the usual manner from left to right, and each book is one inch thick, how far is it from page one of the first book to the last page of the last book?

8. A man buys a car for $500 and sells it for $600. Later, he rebuys the car for $700 and resells it for $800. How much money does he make or lose on the entire transaction?

9. A man drives from Tampa to Ruskin (a distance of thirty miles) at an average speed of thirty miles per hour. How fast must he average on the return trip to average sixty miles per hour for the round trip?

10. A man makes a trip by motorcar at an average speed for the outward journey of thirty miles per hour. On the return trip he averages twenty miles per hour. What is his average speed for the entire trip?

Question: Are these problems suitable for group discussion? Explain.

CASE STUDIES

Directions: The class will be divided into groups of five or six students per group. Each group will discuss the following hypothetical case problems for the alloted time. At the end of the time period, one member from each group will orally report on his group's solution to the problem. Spokesmen should be rotated for each new problem.

1. George, a sophomore, has a freshman friend who works in the lab with him. George has noticed that his friend has "borrowed' several pieces of expensive lab equipment and has never returned them. What should George do? (Five minutes)

2. John is taking a course in math. His average, at the time of the final exam, is a high C. Since the final exam will count 50% toward the total grade, John believes that he has a good chance of getting a B in the course. Just two days before the final, John learns that at least six students have received a copy of the final. One of the group will sell a copy to John for $20. What should John do? (Five minutes)

3. You accidentally bump a car in the parking lot leaving a small dent in the car's right front fender. You have no car insurance. You look around and no one seems to have seen the accident. What do you do? (Ten minutes)

4. Frank, nineteen, and Barbara, eighteen, both students at your school, are living together but are not married. They love each other very much and plan to marry someday and have a family. They learn, to their dismay, that Barbara's mother is coming for a visit. The mother, very strict about Barbara's sexual behavior, thinks that Barbara lives with her girlfriend Frances. If Barbara's mother knew the real situation, she would probably remove Barbara from school. What should Frank and Barbara do? (Ten minutes)

5. You, a college freshman, unexpectedly come into a considerable fortune left to you by a distant relative. You had planned to become a college professor when you finished your schooling. What will you do now that you are wealthy? (Ten minutes)

WHO SHOULD SURVIVE?*

An atomic attack has occurred. The following eleven persons—the only humans alive on earth—are in an atomic bomb shelter. It will take two weeks for the external radiation to drop to a safe level; however, the supplies in the shelter can only sustain seven persons for the two weeks, at a very minimal level. In brief, only seven of the eleven people can survive.

1. Dr. Dane: thirty-seven; white; no religious affiliation; Ph. D. in history; college professor; good health; married; one child (Bobby); active; enjoys politics.
2. Mrs. Dane; thirty-eight; white; Jewish; A.B., M.A. in psychology; mental health counselor; good health; married; one child (Bobby); active in community.
3. Bobby Dane; ten; white; Jewish; special education classes for four years; mentally retarded; I.Q. 70; good health; enjoys his pets.
4. Mrs. Garcia; thirty-three; Spanish-American; Catholic; ninth grade education; cocktail waitress; prostitute; good health; abandoned as a child; in foster home as a youth; attacked by foster father at age twelve; ran away from home; returned to reformatory; stayed until sixteen; married at sixteen; divorced at eighteen; one child three weeks old (Jean).
5. Jean Garcia: three weeks old; Spanish-American; good health; still nursing.
6. Mary Evans: eight; black; Protestant; third grade; good health.
7. Mr. Newton: twenty-five; black; atheist; starting last year of medical school; suspected of homosexual activity; good health; seems bitter about racial problems; wears hippie clothes.
8. Mrs. Clark: twenty-eight; black; Protestant; college graduate; electronic engineer; married; no children; good health; enjoys sports; grew up in ghetto.
9. Mr. Blake: fifty-one; white; Mormon; B.S. in mechanics; very handy; married; four children; good health; enjoys outdoors and working in his shop.
10. Father Frans: thirty-seven; white; Catholic; college plus seminary;

priest; active in civil rights; criticized for liberal views; good health; former college athlete.

11. Dr. Gonzales: sixty-six; Spanish-American; Catholic; doctor in general practice; two heart attacks in past five years; continues to practice medicine.

Problem: Which four of the eleven persons should be ejected from the bomb shelter?

THE ISLAND*

An island, which we shall call Utopia, has been deeded to the Utopian Society of your college by the federal government. The deed offers complete independence to the "owners" of the island and guarantees that the United States will protect the island from state or foreign interference.

There are 500 members in the Utopian Society, all students. Half are women, eighty percent of the students are white and twenty percent are black. The society has agreed to settle on the island within six months and to establish a model utopian community. A federal grant of $1 million has been provided for this purpose. Also, a small 550 ton freighter will be turned over to the group.

The island of Utopia is one hundred miles due west of Bradenton, Florida. It is approximately ten miles long by two miles wide. The island contains an adequate supply of fresh water, has an abundance of tropical fruit, heavy vegetation, and an almost perfect climate year-round. The island has a natural deep-water harbor, and there is an old, dilapidated fifty-room hotel on the harbor. The island is uninhabited, with the exception of wild pigs, small game, and many species of birds.

The class constitutes a Planning Committee of the Utopian Society and has been commissioned by the society to draw up a series of recommendations regarding the political, economic, and social structure of the proposed new community.

Some suggestions for the Planning Committee to consider

1. Determine the long-range goals of the community.

*Reprinted with permission of Macmillan Publishing Co., Inc. from *Communication Games* by Karen R. Krupar. Copyright © 1973 by The Free Press, a Division of Macmillan Publishing Co., Inc.

2. Determine what type of economic system will be adopted: capitalism, socialism, a mixture of those, or something else altogether.
3. What type of governing body will be established?
   a. What officials will be needed? How will they be selected?
   b. What legislative body will be needed? How will the members be selected? What rules or laws will be enacted?
4. How will the community survive economically?
5. What type of social structure will be established? How will it provide for:
   a. Mating? Rearing of children? Education?
   b. Health care?
   c. Religion?
   d. Recreation?
6. What sort of housing will be established? Living arrangements?

YOUR NOTES

DISCUSSION EVALUATION FORM

Name_____

Date _____

Discussion question _____

Participants: (The leader should be listed in the #1 blank and the participants in the remaining blanks in clockwise order from the leader.)

1._____   2._____   3._____

4._____   5._____   6._____

7._____   8._____   9._____

Evaluation of participants: Grade each participant, including the leader, on each item below. One indicates poor; 2, fair; 3, average; 4, good; and 5, excellent.

Participant number 1 2 3 4 5 6 7 8 9
1. Knowledge of subject
2. Analysis of question
3. Use of evidence and reasoning
4. Degree of participation
5. Cooperative attitude
6. Effective speech

Evaluation of leader

	Grades (1–5)
1. Preliminary remarks (introduction)	
2. Guidance of participants	
3. Courtesy and tact	
4. Use of internal summaries	
5. Effective speech	
6. Final summary and conclusion	

Comments and recommendations (Include organization of objectives, use of documented proof, brainstorming techniques, preparation of participants, group effort, group rapport, selection and wording of question, open-mindedness, and willingness to compromise.)

_____

_____

_____

DISCUSSION EVALUATION FORM

Name_____

Date _____

Discussion question _____

Participants: (The leader should be listed in the #1 blank and the participants in the remaining blanks in clockwise order from the leader.)

1._____   2._____   3._____

4._____   5._____   6._____

7._____   8._____   9._____

Evaluation of participants: Grade each participant, including the leader, on each item below. One indicates poor; 2, fair; 3, average; 4, good; and 5, excellent.

Participant number 1 2 3 4 5 6 7 8 9
1. Knowledge of subject
2. Analysis of question
3. Use of evidence and reasoning
4. Degree of participation
5. Cooperative attitude
6. Effective speech

Evaluation of leader

	Grades (1–5)
1. Preliminary remarks (introduction)	
2. Guidance of participants	
3. Courtesy and tact	
4. Use of internal summaries	
5. Effective speech	
6. Final summary and conclusion	

Comments and recommendations (Include organization of objectives, use of documented proof, brainstorming techniques, preparation of participants, group effort, group rapport, selection and wording of question, open-mindedness, and willingness to compromise.)

_____

_____

_____

DISCUSSION EVALUATION FORM

Name_____

Date _____

Discussion question _____

Participants: (The leader should be listed in the #1 blank and the participants in the remaining blanks in clockwise order from the leader.)

1._____ 2._____ 3._____

4._____ 5._____ 6._____

7._____ 8._____ 9._____

Evaluation of participants: Grade each participant, including the leader, on each item below. One indicates poor; 2, fair; 3, average; 4, good; and 5, excellent.

Participant number 1 2 3 4 5 6 7 8 9
1. Knowledge of subject
2. Analysis of question
3. Use of evidence and reasoning
4. Degree of participation
5. Cooperative attitude
6. Effective speech

Evaluation of leader

	Grades (1–5)
1. Preliminary remarks (introduction)	
2. Guidance of participants	
3. Courtesy and tact	
4. Use of internal summaries	
5. Effective speech	
6. Final summary and conclusion	

Comments and recommendations (Include organization of objectives, use of documented proof, brainstorming techniques, preparation of participants, group effort, group rapport, selection and wording of question, open-mindedness, and willingness to compromise.)

_____

_____

_____

DISCUSSION EVALUATION FORM

Name_____

Date _____

Discussion question _____

Participants: (The leader should be listed in the #1 blank and the participants in the remaining blanks in clockwise order from the leader.)

1._____ 2._____ 3._____

4._____ 5._____ 6._____

7._____ 8._____ 9._____

Evaluation of participants: Grade each participant, including the leader, on each item below. One indicates poor; 2, fair; 3, average; 4, good; and 5, excellent.

Participant number 1 2 3 4 5 6 7 8 9
1. Knowledge of subject
2. Analysis of question
3. Use of evidence and reasoning
4. Degree of participation
5. Cooperative attitude
6. Effective speech

Evaluation of leader

Grades (1–5)

1. Preliminary remarks (introduction)

2. Guidance of participants

3. Courtesy and tact

4. Use of internal summaries

5. Effective speech

6. Final summary and conclusion

Comments and recommendations (Include organization of objectives, use of documented proof, brainstorming techniques, preparation of participants, group effort, group rapport, selection and wording of question, open-mindedness, and willingness to compromise.)

DISCUSSION INTERACTION CHART

Group_____ Name _____

Date_____

Directions: The numbers below represent the members of the discussion group. Number 1 is the moderator and the others are the participants, in clockwise order from the moderator. Indicate each spoken contribution by order, under the member making it. For example, if the moderator (#1) makes the first contribution, place a 1 in the moderator's square. If participant #5 makes the second contribution, place a 2 in the #5 square. New squares should be used for each ten-minute segment of the discussion. If a contribution is especially valuable, indicate this numeral with a plus sign. When totalling the contributions for each member, consider a plus numeral one-and-a-half contributions.

Time	1	2	3	4	5	6	7
First 10 minutes							
Second 10 minutes							
Third 10 minutes							
Fourth 10 minutes							
Fifth 10 minutes							
Total							

Discussion members:　1.＿＿＿＿＿＿＿＿＿　2.＿＿＿＿＿＿＿＿＿

3.＿＿＿＿＿＿＿＿＿　4.＿＿＿＿＿＿＿＿＿　5.＿＿＿＿＿＿＿＿＿

6.＿＿＿＿＿＿＿＿＿　7.＿＿＿＿＿＿＿＿＿

Comment on the leader's and participants' contributions, the attitude of members towards teamwork, and their knowledge of the subject.

＿＿＿＿＿＿＿＿＿＿＿＿＿＿＿＿＿＿＿＿＿＿＿＿＿＿＿＿＿＿＿＿

＿＿＿＿＿＿＿＿＿＿＿＿＿＿＿＿＿＿＿＿＿＿＿＿＿＿＿＿＿＿＿＿

＿＿＿＿＿＿＿＿＿＿＿＿＿＿＿＿＿＿＿＿＿＿＿＿＿＿＿＿＿＿＿＿

＿＿＿＿＿＿＿＿＿＿＿＿＿＿＿＿＿＿＿＿＿＿＿＿＿＿＿＿＿＿＿＿

DISCUSSION INTERACTION CHART

Group _____ Name _____

Date _____

Directions: The numbers below represent the members of the discussion group. Number 1 is the moderator and the others are the participants, in clockwise order from the moderator. Indicate each spoken contribution by order, under the member making it. For example, if the moderator (#1) makes the first contribution, place a 1 in the moderator's square. If participant #5 makes the second contribution, place a 2 in the #5 square. New squares should be used for each ten-minute segment of the discussion. If a contribution is especially valuable, indicate this numeral with a plus sign. When totalling the contributions for each member, consider a plus numeral one-and-and-a-half contributions.

Time	1	2	3	4	5	6	7
First 10 minutes							
Second 10 minutes							
Third 10 minutes							
Fourth 10 minutes							
Fifth 10 minutes							
Total							

Discussion members: 1._____   2._____

3._____   4._____   5._____

6._____   7._____

Comment on the leader's and participants' contributions, the attitude of members towards teamwork, and their knowledge of the subject.

_____

_____

_____

_____

DISCUSSION INTERACTION CHART

Group_____   Name _____

Date _____

Directions: The numbers below represent the members of the discussion group. Number 1 is the moderator and the others are the participants, in clockwise order from the moderator. Indicate each spoken contribution by order, under the member making it. For example, if the moderator (#1) makes the first contribution, place a 1 in the moderator's square. If participant #5 makes the second contribution, place a 2 in the #5 square. New squares should be used for each ten-minute segment of the discussion. If a contribution is especially valuable, indicate this numeral with a plus sign. When totalling the contributions for each member, consider a plus numeral one-and-a-half contributions.

Time	1	2	3	4	5	6	7
First 10 minutes							
Second 10 minutes							
Third 10 minutes							
Fourth 10 minutes							
Fifth 10 minutes							
Total							

Discussion members: 1._____   2._____

3._____   4._____   5._____

6._____   7._____

Comment on the leader's and participants' contributions, the attitude of members towards teamwork, and their knowledge of the subject.

_____

_____

_____

_____

DISCUSSION INTERACTION CHART

Group_____   Name _____

Date _____

Directions: The numbers below represent the members of the discussion group. Number 1 is the moderator and the others are the participants, in clockwise order from the moderator. Indicate each spoken contribution by order, under the member making it. For example, if the moderator (#1) makes the first contribution, place a 1 in the moderator's square. If participant #5 makes the second contribution, place a 2 in the #5 square. New squares should be used for each ten-minute segment of the discussion. If a contribution is especially valuable, indicate this numeral with a plus sign. When totalling the contributions for each member, consider a plus numeral one-and-a-half contributions.

Time	1	2	3	4	5	6	7
First 10 minutes							
Second 10 minutes							
Third 10 minutes							
Fourth 10 minutes							
Fifth 10 minutes							
Total							

Discussion members: 1._____   2._____

3._____   4._____   5._____

6._____   7._____

Comment on the leader's and participants' contributions, the attitude of members towards teamwork, and their knowledge of the subject.

_____

_____

_____

_____

SPEECH OUTLINE

Subject _____   Name _____

Specific Purpose _____   Date _____

I. Introduction
   A. Attention step. (Gain attention and indicate topic.)
   B. Motivation step. (Tell why subject is important to audience.)
   C. Purpose sentence.
II. Body
   A. First major statement.
      1. Supporting statement.
         a. Sub-point.
         b. Sub-point.
      2. Supporting statement.
         a. Sub-point.
         b. Sub-point.
   B. Second major statement.
III. Conclusion

Sources: (title, author, publisher, date, and page number.)

Note: Your outline should include all these elements, including sub-points. The introduction and conclusion should be written exactly as you will deliver them. All other material should be expressed in complete sentences or complete ideas.

YOUR SPEECH OUTLINE

OCCASION AND AUDIENCE ANALYSIS

Name _____

Date _____

I. Occasion Analysis

   A. Date and time of speech _____

   B. Meeting place; address_____

      1. Size of room_____
         a. Facilities: Microphone, lectern, blackboard, electric outlets.

   C. Sponsor of the meeting; chairperson_____

   D. Purpose of meeting_____

   E. Order of program; other speakers _____

      _____

   F. Time limits of your talk. Maximum_____Minimum _____
II. Audience Analysis

   A. Approximate size of audience _____

   B. Age of audience; adults, youth, children, mixes _____

   C. Sex of audience_____

   D. Educational, vocational, economic background_____

      _____

   E. Special interests, attitudes, prejudices, political leanings_____

      _____

    F. Probable purpose in attending meeting _____

                              _____

  III. Speech Subject and Specific Purpose. (On basis of above analysis)

    A. Subject _____

    B. Purpose _____

SPEECH CRITICISM GUIDE

1. What was the specific purpose of the speech? To what extent was the purpose accomplished?

2. What verbal device was used to capture attention? Was it effective? How could it be improved?

3. How did the speaker motivate the audience? How effective was the motivation? How else could the speech have been motivated?

4. Was the speaker's appearance (poise, posture and dress) appropriate for the occasion? Give your recommendations.

5. Comment on the adequacy of each of the following:
   a. loudness
   b. rate
   c. variety of pitch, rate, and loudness
   d. pronunciation and clarity of articulation
   e. audience contact
   f. extemporaneous style
   g. gesture and movement on the platform
   h. Dynamic presentation

6. Did the speaker appear to know the subject thoroughly? Was the speaker authoritative?

7. What speech supporting devices did the speaker use? Were the devices adequate? What additional speech supports could have been used effectively?

8. If the speech was persuasive in purpose, was the evidence adequate? Sources given? Was reasoning adequate for the conclusions drawn? Were there fallacies of any type?

9. What type of conclusion did the speaker use? Was it effective?

10. What was the total impact of the speech on you? Was your curiosity aroused? Were your attitudes or beliefs modified? Explain.

YOUR SPEECH CRITICISM

SPEAKER ANALYSIS

The following guide can be used with the Speech Criticism Guide to prepare a written evaluation of a speaker.

Speaker
(Name and title)_____

Name_____

Date _____

Place (Include address)_____

_____

Occasion _____

Subject_____

I. Outline of speech content
II. Analyze the speech content. Include whether the speaker used examples, definitions, quotations, statistics, or slogans.
III. Analyze the delivery. Comment on the method of gaining attention, motivating the audience, and the purpose sentence. Comment on poise, posture, use of gesture, bodily movement, loudness, rate, vocal variety, eye contact, pronunciation, enthusiasm, and authoritativeness.
IV. Describe the audience reaction. Indicate the probable effect of the speaker on the audience: approval, belief, acceptance, or rejection.
V. Recommendations. Give your detailed suggestions on how the speech could have been improved.

YOUR SPEAKER ANALYSIS

SPEECH EVALUATION CHART

Name _____

Date _____

Speech Factor Grading: 1 (poor) to 5 (excellent)	Grade
Introduction (attention, motivation, purpose)	
Visible factors (appearance, poise, movement, gestures)	
Audience contact	
Vocal factors (pitch, rate, loudness, vocal variety)	
Knowledge of subject matter	
Organization of subject matter	
Vocabulary and word choice	
Extemporaneous style	
Enthusiasm	
Conclusion	

Comments _____

_____

_____

_____

Recommendations _____

_____

_____

_____

SPEECH EVALUATION CHART

Name _____

Date _____

Speech Factor Grading: 1 (poor) to 5 (excellent)	Grade
Introduction (attention, motivation, purpose)	
Visible factors (appearance, poise, movement, gestures)	
Audience contact	
Vocal factors (pitch, rate, loudness, vocal variety)	
Knowledge of subject matter	
Organization of subject matter	
Vocabulary and word choice	
Extemporaneous style	
Enthusiasm	
Conclusion	

Comments _____

_____

_____

_____

Recommendations _____

_____

_____

_____

SPEECH EVALUATION CHART

Name _____

Date _____

Speech Factor Grading: 1 (poor) to 5 (excellent)	Grade
Introduction (attention, motivation, purpose)	
Visible factors (appearance, poise, movement, gestures)	
Audience contact	
Vocal factors (pitch, rate, loudness, vocal variety)	
Knowledge of subject matter	
Organization of subject matter	
Vocabulary and word choice	
Extemporaneous style	
Enthusiasm	
Conclusion	

Comments _____

_____

_____

_____

Recommendations _____

_____

_____

_____

SPEECH EVALUATION CHART

Name _____

Date _____

Speech Factor Grading: 1 (poor) to 5 (excellent)	Grade
Introduction (attention, motivation, purpose)	
Visible factors (appearance, poise, movement, gestures)	
Audience contact	
Vocal factors (pitch, rate, loudness, vocal variety)	
Knowledge of subject matter	
Organization of subject matter	
Vocabulary and word choice	
Extemporaneous style	
Enthusiasm	
Conclusion	

Comments _____

_____

_____

_____

Recommendations _____

_____

_____

_____

SPEECH EVALUATION CHART

Name _____

Date _____

Speech Factor Grading: 1 (poor) to 5 (excellent)	Grade
Introduction (attention, motivation, purpose)	
Visible factors (appearance, poise, movement, gestures)	
Audience contact	
Vocal factors (pitch, rate, loudness, vocal variety)	
Knowledge of subject matter	
Organization of subject matter	
Vocabulary and word choice	
Extemporaneous style	
Enthusiasm	
Conclusion	

Comments _____

_____

_____

_____

Recommendations _____

_____

_____

_____

SPEECH EVALUATION CHART

Name _____

Date _____

Speech Factor Grading: 1 (poor) to 5 (excellent)	Grade
Introduction (attention, motivation, purpose)	
Visible factors (appearance, poise, movement, gestures)	
Audience contact	
Vocal factors (pitch, rate, loudness, vocal variety)	
Knowledge of subject matter	
Organization of subject matter	
Vocabulary and word choice	
Extemporaneous style	
Enthusiasm	
Conclusion	

Comments _____

_____

_____

_____

Recommendations _____

_____

_____

_____

PRESIDENT CARTER'S ADDRESS TO THE UNITED NATIONS

March 17, 1977

I am proud to be with you tonight in this house where the shared hopes of mankind can find a voice.

I have come here to express my own support, and the continuing support of my country, for the ideals of the United Nations.

We are proud that, for the thirty-two years since its creation, the United Nations has met on American soil. And we share with you the commitments to freedom, self-government, human dignity, mutual toleration and peaceful resolution of disputes which the founding principles of the United Nations and Secretary General Kurt Waldheim so well represent.

No one nation can by itself build a world which reflects these values. But the United States has a reservoir of strength—economic strength, which we are willing to share; military strength, which we hope never again to have to use; and the strength of ideals, which we are determined fully to maintain as the backbone of our foreign policy.

It is now eight weeks since I became President. I have brought to office a firm commitment to a more open foreign policy. I believe that the American people expect me to speak frankly about the policies we intend to pursue and it is in that spirit that I speak to you tonight about our hopes for the future.

I see a hopeful world, a world dominated by increasing demands for basic freedoms, for fundamental rights, for higher standards of human existence. We are eager to take part in the shaping of this world.

But in speaking of such a better world, we are not blind to the reality of disagreement nor to the persisting dangers that confront us. Every headline reminds us of bitter divisions, of national hostilities, of territorial conflicts, of ideological competition. In the Middle East peace is a quarter of a century overdue. A gathering racial conflict threatens Southern Africa, new tensions are rising in the horn of Africa; disputes in the eastern Mediterranean remain to be resolved.

Perhaps even more ominous is the staggering arms race. The Soviet Union and the United States have accumulated thousands of nuclear weapons. Our two nations have almost five times as many missile warheads today as we had eight years ago. Yet we are not five times more secure! On the contrary, the arms race has only increased the risk of conflict.

We can only improve this world if we are realistic about its complexities. The disagreements we face are deeply rooted and they often raise difficult philosophical as well as practical issues. They will not be solved easily nor quickly. The arms race is now imbedded in the fabric of international affairs and can only be contained with the greatest of difficulty. Poverty and inequality are of such monumental scope that it will take decades of deliberate and determined effort even to improve the situation.

I stress these dangers and these difficulties because I want all of us to dedicate ourselves to a prolonged and persistent effort designed

To maintain peace and to reduce the arms race.

To help build a better and more cooperative international economic system.

To work with potential adversaries as well as with our friends to advance the cause of human rights.

In seeking these goals, I recognize that the United States cannot solve the problems of the world. We can sometimes help others resolve their differences, but we cannot do so by imposing our own particular solutions.

In the coming months, there is important work for all of us in advancing international cooperation and economic progress in the cause of peace:

Later this spring the leaders of several industrial nations of Europe, North America, and Japan will confer at a Summit meeting in London on a broad range of issues. We must promote the health of our industrial economies, seek to restrain inflation, and begin to find ways of managing our domestic economies for the benefit of the global economy.

We must move forward with the multilateral trade negotiations in Geneva.

The United States will support the efforts of our friends to strengthen democratic institutions in Europe, particularly in Portugal and Spain.

We will work closely with our European friends on the forthcoming Review Conference on Security and Cooperation in Europe. We want to make certain that all provisions of the Helsinki agreement are fully implemented and that progress is made to further East–West cooperation.

In the Middle East we are doing our best to clarify areas of agreement, to surface underlying consensus, and to help develop mutually acceptable principles which can form a flexible framework for a just and permanent settlement.

In Southern Africa we will work to help attain majority rule through peaceful means. We believe that such fundamental transformation can be achieved, to the advantage of both blacks and whites. Anything less than that may bring a protracted racial war, with devastating consequences for all. This week the government of the United States took action to bring our country into full compliance with United Nations sanctions against the illegal regime in Rhodesia.

We will put our relations with Latin America on a more constructive footing, recognizing the global character of the region's problems. We are also working to resolve in amicable negotiations the future of the Panama Canal.

We will continue our efforts to develop further our relationship with the People's Republic of China. We recognize our parallel strategic interests in maintaining stability in Asia and will act in the spirit of the Shanghai communiqué.

In Southeast Asia and the Pacific we will strengthen our association with our traditional friends and seek to improve relations with our former adversaries.

Throughout the world, we are ready to normalize our relations and seek reconciliation with all states which are ready to work with us in promoting global progress.

Above all, the search for peace requires a much more deliberate effort to contain the global arms race. Let me speak in this context first of the U.S.–Soviet relationship, and then of the wider need to contain the proliferation of arms throughout the global community.

I intend to pursue the strategic arms limitation talks between the United States and the Soviet Union with determination and with energy. SALT is extraordinarily complicated. But the basic fact is that while the negotiations remain deadlocked the arms race goes on, the security of both countries and the entire world is threatened. My preference would be for strict controls or even a freeze on new types and new generations of weaponry, with a deep reduction in the strategic arms of both sides. Such a major step towards not only arms limitations but arms reductions would be welcomed by mankind as a giant step towards peace.

Alternatively, and perhaps more easily, we could conclude a more limited agreement based on those elements of the Vladivostok accord on which we can find consensus, and set aside for prompt consideration and subsequent negotiations the more contentious issues and also the deeper reductions that I favor.

We will also explore the possiblity of a total cessation of nuclear testing. While our ultimate goal is for all nuclear powers to end testing, we do not regard this as a prerequisite for suspension of tests by the two prinicpal nuclear powers. We should, however, also pursue a broad and permanent multilateral agreement on this issue.

We will also seek to establish Soviet willingness to reach agreement with us on mutual military restraint in the Indian Ocean, as well as on such matters as arms exports to troubled areas of the world.

In proposing such accommodations I remain fully aware that American–Soviet relations will continue to be highly competitive, but I believe that our competition must be balanced by cooperation in preserving peace, and thus our mutual survival. I will seek such cooperation earnestly and sincerely.

However, the effort to contain the arms race is not a matter just for the United States and the Soviet Union alone. There must be a wider effort to reduce the flow of weapons to all the troubled spots of this globe. Accordingly, we will try to reach broader agreements among producer and consumer nations to limit the export of conventional arms, and we will take initiatives of our own since the United States has become one of the major arms suppliers of the world.

We are deeply committed to halting the proliferation of nuclear weapons among the nations of the world. We will undertake a new effort to reach multilateral agreements designed to provide legitimate supplies of nuclear fuels while controlling poisonous and dangerous atomic wastes.

Working with other nations represented here, we hope thus to advance the cause of peace. We will make a strong and positive contribution to the upcoming special session on disarmament.

But the search for peace also means the search for justice. One of the greatest challenges before us as a nation, and therefore one of our greatest opportunities, is to participate in molding a global economic system which will bring greater prosperity to the people of all countries.

I come from a part of the United States which is largely agrarian and which for many years did not have the advantages of adequate transportation, capital, management skills, education, which were available in the industrial states of our country. So I can sympathize with the leaders of the developing nations, and I want them to know that we will do our part.

To this end the United States will be advancing proposals aimed at meeting the basic human needs of the developing world and helping them to increase their productive capacity. I have asked Congress to provide $7.5 billion of foreign assistance in the coming year, and I will work to insure sustained American assistance as the process of global economic development continues. I am also urging the Congress to increase our contributions to the United Nations Development Program and meet in full our pledges to multilateral lending institutions, especially the International Development Association of the World Bank.

We remain committed to an open international trading system, one which does not ignore domestic concerns in the United States. We have extended duty-free treatment to many products from the developing countries. In the multilateral trade negotiations in Geneva we have offered substantial trade concessions on goods of primary interest to developing countries. In accordance with the Tokyo declaration, we are also examining ways to provide additional consideration for the special needs of developing countries.

The United States is willing to consider, with a positive and open attitude, the negotiation of agreements to stabilize commodity prices, including the establishment of a common funding arrangement for financing buffer stocks where they are a part of individual negotiated agreements.

I also believe that the developing countries must acquire fuller participation in the global economic decision-making process. Some progress has been made in this regard by expanding participation of developing countries in the International Monetary Fund.

We must use our collective natural resources wisely and constructively. Today our oceans are being plundered and defiled. With a renewed spirit of cooperation and hope we join in the Conference of the Law of the Sea in order to correct the mistakes of past generations and to insure that all nations can share the bounties of the eternal seas.

We must also recognize that the world is facing serious shortages of energy. This is a truly global problem. For our part, we are determined to reduce waste and to work with others towards a proper sharing of the benefits and costs of energy resources.

The search for peace and justice means also respect for human dignity. All the signatories of the U.N. Charter have pledged themselves to observe and respect basic human rights. Thus, no member of the United Nations can claim that mistreatment of its citizens is solely its own business. Equally, no member can avoid its responsibilities to review and to speak when torture or unwarranted deprivation of freedom occurs in any part of the world.

The basic thrust of human affairs points toward a more universal demand for fundamental human rights. The United States has a historical birthright to be associated with this process.

We in the United States accept this responsibility in the fullest and most constructive sense. Ours is a commitment, not just a political posture. I know perhaps as well as anyone that our ideals in the area of human rights have not always been attained in the United States, but the American people have an abiding commitment to the full realization of these ideals. We are determined therefore, to deal with our deficiencies quickly and openly.

Action on U. N. Covenants

To demonstrate this commitment I will seek Congressional approval and sign the U.N. covenants on economic, social, and cultural rights, and the covenant on civil and political rights. I will work closely with our Congress in seeking its support to ratify not only these two instruments, but the United National Genocide Convention and the Treaty for the Elimination of All Forms of Racial Discrimination as well. I have just removed the last remaining restrictions to American travel abroad and will move to liberalize travel opportunities to America.

The United Nations is the global forum dedicated to the peace and well-being of every individual—no matter how weak or how poor. But we have allowed its human-rights machinery to be ignored and sometimes politicized. There is much that can be done to strengthen it.

The Human Rights Commission should be prepared to meet more often, and all nations should be prepared to offer it their fullest cooperation—to welcome its investigations, to work with its officials, to act on its reports.

I would like to see the entire U.N. Human Rights Division moved back here to the central headquarters, where its activities will be in the forefront of our attention and where the attention of the press corps can stimulate us to deal honestly with this sensitive issue. The proposal made twelve years ago by the Government of Costa Rica—to establish a U.N. High Commissioner for Human Rights—also deserves our renewed attention and support.

Strengthened international machinery will help us all to close the gap between promise and performance in protecting human rights. When gross or widespread violation takes place—contrary to international commitments—it is the concern of all. The solemn commitments of the U.N. Charter, of the U.N.'s Universal Declaration of Human Rights, of the Helsinki accords and of many other international instruments must be taken just as seriously as commercial or security agreements.

The issue is important by itself. It should not block progress on other important matters affecting the security and well-being of our people and of world peace. It is obvious that the reduction of tension, the control of nuclear arms, the achievement of harmony in troubled areas of the world, and the provision of food, good health, and education will independently contribute to advancing the human condition.

In our relations with other countries these mutual concerns will be reflected in our political, our cultural, and our economic attitudes.

These then are our basic priorities as we work with other members to strengthen and to improve the United Nations:

We will strive for peace in the troubled areas of the world.
We will aggressively seek to control the weaponry of war.
We will promote a new system of international economic progress and cooperation; and
We will be steadfast in our dedication to the dignity and well-being of people throughout the world.

I believe this is a foreign policy that is consistent with America's historic values and commitments. I believe it is a foreign policy that is consonant with the ideals of the United Nations.

Thank you.

Index

317